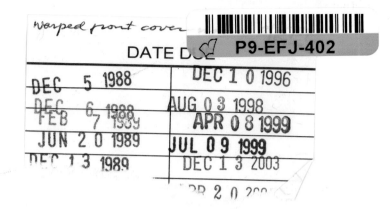

ARTHUR MILLER

Modern Critical Views

These and other titles in preparation

Modern Critical Views

ARTHUR MILLER

Edited and with an introduction by
Harold Bloom
Sterling Professor of the Humanities
Yale University

CHELSEA HOUSE PUBLISHERS ◇ 1987
New York ◇ New Haven ◇ Philadelphia

© 1987 by Chelsea House Publishers,
a division of Chelsea House Educational Communications, Inc.,
   95 Madison Avenue, New York, NY 10016
   345 Whitney Avenue, New Haven, CT 06511
   5014 West Chester Pike, Edgemont, PA 19028

Introduction © 1987 by Harold Bloom

Printed and bound in the United States of America

∞ The paper used in this publication meets the minimum
requirements of the American National Standard for
Permanence of Paper for Printed Library Materials,
Z39.48-1984.

Library of Congress Cataloging-in-Publication Data

Arthur Miller.

   (Modern critical views)
   Bibliography: p.
   Includes index.
   Contents: Arthur Miller / Raymond Williams—Strength and
weakness in Arthur Miller / Tom F. Driver—Death of a
salesman / Esther Merle Jackson—[etc.]
   1. Miller, Arthur, 1915–   —Criticism and interpretation. [1.
Miller, Arthur, 1915–   —Criticism and interpretation. 2.
American drama—History and criticism] I. Bloom, Harold.
II. Series.
PS3525.I5156Z514   1987   812'.52   86-29962
ISBN 0-87754-711-4 (alk. paper)

Contents

Editor's Note

This book gathers together what I consider to be the most useful criticism available upon the plays of Arthur Miller, arranged in the chronological order of its original publication. I am grateful to Edward Jefferson and Henry Finder for their aid in researching this volume.

My introduction centers upon *All My Sons* and *Death of a Salesman*, and seeks to define how both plays, particularly the latter, achieve aesthetic dignity despite Miller's limitations as a writer. The chronological sequence of criticism begins with an overview by the distinguished Marxist critic, Raymond Williams, which relates Miller's work to the tradition of expressionism in modern drama. Tom F. Driver finds Miller's strength to be in his capacity for publicly addressing his audience, while Miller's weakness is located in a moralism that has no coherent idea of the good.

Studying *Death of a Salesman*, Esther Merle Jackson attempts to set Willy Loman in the context of ancient tragic myths that became drama. Whether Loman does not hover between pathos and tragedy, with every other protagonist in Miller, is the question addressed by Clinton W. Trowbridge. Orm Överland chronicles Miller's uneasy departures from realistic conventions in drama, and suggests that Miller is valuable only when he works in the forms of realism.

After the Fall, a problematical play, is read by Dennis Welland as Miller's drama of self-forgiveness. Leonard Moss, examining the social perspective that is Miller's one thematic resource, argues in an overview that Miller's aesthetic success, despite its clear limitations, remains considerable. Centering upon *A View from the Bridge,* Neil Carson emphasizes Miller's preference for the direct communication of passion to the audience.

In a retrospective estimate, C. W. E. Bigsby praises Miller for engaging directly with the fears, anxieties, dreams of the American people, still desperate to believe in a freedom they find perpetually vanishing before them. E. Miller Budick concludes this volume with a consideration of *The Crucible,* Miller's allegorical drama of witch-hunting, which is seen here as a quest into history in order to uncover the core reasons for human sinfulness, reasons that for Miller include our guilt and our pride.

Introduction

Rather like Eugene O'Neill before him, Arthur Miller raises, at least for me, the difficult critical question as to whether there is not an element in drama that is other than literary, even contrary in value (supposed or real) to literary values, perhaps even to aesthetic values. O'Neill, a very nearly great dramatist, particularly in *The Iceman Cometh* and *Long Day's Journey into Night,* is not a good writer, except perhaps in his stage directions. Miller is by no means a bad writer, but he is scarcely an eloquent master of the language. I have just reread *All My Sons, Death of a Salesman,* and *The Crucible,* and am compelled to reflect how poorly they reread, though all of them, properly staged, are very effective dramas, and *Death of a Salesman* is considerably more than that. It ranks with *Iceman, Long Day's Journey,* Williams's *A Streetcar Named Desire,* Wilder's *The Skin of Our Teeth* and Albee's *The Zoo Story* as one of the half-dozen crucial American plays. Yet its literary status seems to me somewhat questionable, which returns me to the issue of what there is in drama that can survive indifferent or even poor writing.

Defending *Death of a Salesman,* despite what he admits is a sentimental glibness in its prose, Kenneth Tynan memorably observed: "But the theater is an impure craft, and *Death of a Salesman* organizes its impurities with an emotional effect unrivalled in postwar drama." The observation still seems true, a quarter-century after Tynan made it, yet how unlikely a similar statement would seem if ventured about Ibsen, Miller's prime precursor. Do we speak of *Hedda Gabler* organizing its impurities with an unrivalled emotional effect? Why is the American drama, except for Thornton Wilder (its one great sport), addicted to an organization of impurities, a critical phrase perhaps applicable only to Theodore Dreiser, among the major American novelists? Why is it that we have brought forth *The Scarlet Letter, Moby-Dick, Adventures of Huckleberry Finn, The Portrait of a Lady, The Sun Also Rises, The Great Gatsby, As I Lay Dying, Miss Lonelyhearts, The*

1

Crying of Lot 49, but no comparable dramas? How can a nation whose poets include Whitman, Dickinson, Frost, Stevens, Eliot, Hart Crane, Elizabeth Bishop, James Merrill and John Ashbery, among so many others of the highest aesthetic dignity—how can it offer us only O'Neill, Miller, and Williams as its strongest playwrights?

Drama at its most eminent tends not to appear either too early or too late in any national literature. The United States may be the great exception, since before O'Neill we had little better than Clyde Fitch, and our major dramas (it is to be hoped) have not yet manifested themselves. I have seen little speculation upon this matter, with the grand exception of Alvin B. Kernan, the magisterial scholarly critic of Shakespeare and of Elizabethan dramatic literature. Meditating upon American plays, in 1967, Kernan tuned his initially somber notes to hopeful ones:

> Thus with all our efforts, money, and good intentions, we have not yet achieved a theater; and we have not, I believe, because we do not see life in historic and dramatic terms. Even our greatest novelists and poets, sensitive and subtle though they are, do not think dramatically, and should not be asked to, for they express themselves and us in other forms more suited to their visions (and ours). But we have come very close at moments to having great plays, if not a great theatrical tradition. When the Tyrone family stands in its parlor looking at the mad mother holding her wedding dress and knowing that all the good will in the world cannot undo what the past has done to them; when Willy Loman, the salesman, plunges again and again into the past to search for the point where it all went irremediably wrong and cannot find any one fatal turning point; when the Antrobus family, to end on a more cheerful note, drafts stage hands from backstage to take the place of sick actors, gathers its feeble and ever-disappointed hopes, puts its miserable home together again after another in a series of unending disasters stretching from the ice age to the present; then we are very close to accepting our entanglement in the historical process and our status as actors, which may in time produce a true theater.

That time has not yet come, twenty years later, but I think that Kernan was more right even than he knew. Our greatest novelists and poets continue not to see life in historic and dramatic terms, precisely because our literary tradition remains incurably Emersonian, and Emerson shrewdly dismissed both history and drama as European rather than American. An overtly anti-Emersonian poet-novelist like Robert Penn Warren does see life in historic and dramatic terms, and yet has done his best work away from the stage, despite his effort to write *All the King's Men* as a play. Our foremost novelist, Henry James, failed as a dramatist, precisely because he was more Emersonian than he knew, and turned too far inward in nuanced vision for a play to be his proper mode of representation. One hardly sees Faulkner or Frost, Hemingway or Stevens as dramatists, though they all made their attempts. Nor would a comparison of *The Waste Land* and *The Family Reunion* be kind to Eliot's dramatic ambitions. The American literary mode, whether narrative or lyric, tends towards romance and rumination, or fantastic vision, rather than drama. Emerson, genius of the shores of America, directed us away from history, and distrusted drama as a revel. Nothing is got for nothing; Faulkner and Wallace Stevens, aesthetic light-years beyond O'Neill and Tennessee Williams, seem to mark the limits of the literary imagination in our American century. It is unfair to *All My Sons* and *Death of a Salesman* to read them with the high expectations we rightly bring to *As I Lay Dying* and *Notes Toward a Supreme Fiction*. Miller, a social dramatist, keenly aware of history, fills an authentic American need, certainly for his own time.

II

All My Sons (1947), Miller's first success, retains the flavor of post-World War II America, though it is indubitably something beyond a period piece. Perhaps all of Miller's work could be titled *The Guilt of the Fathers*, which is a dark matter for a Jewish playwright, brought up to believe in the normative tradition, with its emphasis upon the virtues of the fathers. Though it is a truism to note that *All My Sons* is an Ibsenite play, the influence relation to Ibsen remains authentic, and is part of the play's meaning, in the sense that Ibsen too is one of the fathers, and shares in their guilt. Ibsen's peculiar guilt in *All My Sons* is to have appropriated most of Miller's available stock of dramatic language. The result is that this drama is admirably constructed yet not adequately expressed. It is not just that eloquence is lacking; sometimes the characters seem unable to say what they need to say if we are to be with them as we should.

Joe Keller ought to be the hero-villain of *All My Sons*, since pragmatically he certainly is a villain. But Miller is enormously fond of Joe, and so are we; he is not a good man, and yet he lives like one, in regard to family, friends, neighbors. I do not think that Miller ever is interested in Hannah Arendt's curious notion of the banality of evil. Joe is banal, and he is not

evil, though his business has led him into what must be called moral idiocy,
in regard to his partner, and to any world that transcends his own immediate family. Poor Joe is just not very intelligent, and it is Miller's curious
gift that he can render such a man dramatically interesting. An ordinary
man who wants to have a moderately good time, who wants his family
never to suffer, and who lacks any imagination beyond the immediate: what
is this except an authentic American Everyman? The wretched Joe simply is
someone who does not know enough, indeed who scarcely knows anything
at all. Nor can he learn anything. What I find least convincing in the play is
Joe's moment of breaking through to a moral awareness, and a new kind of
knowledge:

> MOTHER: Why are you going? You'll sleep, why are you going?
> KELLER: I can't sleep here. I'll feel better if I go.
> MOTHER: You're so foolish. Larry was your son too, wasn't he?
>   You know he'd never tell you to do this.
> KELLER, *looking at letter in his hand:* Then what is this if it isn't
>   telling me? Sure, he was my son. But I think to him they
>   were all my sons. And I guess they were, I guess they were.
>   I'll be right down. *Exits into house.*
> MOTHER, *to Chris, with determination:* You're not going to take
>   him!
> CHRIS: I'm taking him.
> MOTHER: It's up to you, if you tell him to stay he'll stay. Go and
>   tell him!
> CHRIS: Nobody could stop him now.
> MOTHER: You'll stop him! How long will he live in prison? Are
>   you trying to kill him?

Nothing in Joe is spiritually capable of seeing and saying: "They were
all my sons. And I guess they were, I guess they were." That does not reverberate any more persuasively than Chris crying out: "There's a universe
of people outside and you're responsible to it." Drama fails Miller there, or
perhaps he fails drama. Joe Keller was too remote from a felt sense of reality
for Miller to represent the estrangement properly, except in regard to the
blindness Joe manifested towards his two sons. Miller crossed over into his
one permanent achievement when he swerved from Ibsen into the marginal
world of *Death of a Salesman*, where the pain is the meaning, and the
meaning has a repressed but vital relationship to the normative vision that
informs Jewish memory.

III

The strength of *Death of a Salesman* may be puzzling, and yet is beyond dispute; the continued vitality of the play cannot be questioned. Whether it has the aesthetic dignity of tragedy is not clear, but no other American play is worthier of the term, so far. I myself resist the drama each time I reread it, because it seems that its language will not hold me, and then I see it played on stage, most recently by Dustin Hoffman, and I yield to it. Miller has caught an American kind of suffering that is also a universal mode of pain, quite possibly because his hidden paradigm for his American tragedy is an ancient Jewish one. Willy Loman is hardly a biblical figure, and he is not supposed to be Jewish, yet something crucial in him is Jewish, and the play does belong to that undefined entity we can call Jewish literature, just as Pinter's *The Caretaker* rather surprisingly does. The only meaning of Willy Loman is the pain he suffers, and the pain his fate causes us to suffer. His tragedy makes sense only in the Freudian world of repression, which happens also to be the world of normative Jewish memory. It is a world in which everything has already happened, in which there never can be anything new again, because there is total sense or meaningfulness in everything, which is to say, in which everything hurts.

That cosmos informed by Jewish memory is the secret strength or permanent coherence of *Death of a Salesman,* and accounts for its ability to withstand the shrewd critique of Eric Bentley, who found that the genres of tragedy and of social drama destroyed one another here. Miller's passionate insistence upon tragedy is partly justified by Willy's perpetual sense of being in exile. Commenting on his play, Miller wrote that: "The truly valueless man, a man without ideals, is always perfectly at home anywhere." But Willy, in his own small but valid way, has his own version of the Nietzschean "desire to be elsewhere, the desire to be different," and it does reduce to a Jewish version. Doubtless, as Mary McCarthy first noted, Willy "could not be Jewish because he had to be American." Nearly forty years later, that distinction is pragmatically blurred, and we can wonder if the play might be stronger if Willy were more overtly Jewish.

We first hear Willy say: "It's all right. I came back." His last utterance is the mere repetition of the desperately hushing syllable: "Shhh!" just before he rushes out to destroy himself. A survivor who no longer desires to survive is something other than a tragic figure. Willy, hardly a figure of capable imagination, nevertheless is a representation of terrible pathos. Can we define precisely what that pathos is?

Probably the most famous speech in *Death of a Salesman* is Linda's pre-elegy for her husband, of whom she is soon to remark: "A small man can be just as exhausted as a great man." The plangency of Linda's lament has a universal poignance, even if we wince at its naked design upon us:

> Willy Loman never made a lot of money. His name was never in the paper. He's not the finest character that ever lived. But he's a human being, and a terrible thing is happening to him. So attention must be paid. He's not to be allowed to fall into his grave like an old dog. Attention, attention must be finally paid to such a person.

Behind this is Miller's belated insistence "that everyone knew Willy Loman," which is a flawed emphasis on Miller's part, since he first thought of calling the play *The Inside of His Head,* and Willy already lives in a phantasmagoria when the drama opens. You cannot know a man half lost in the American dream, a man who is unable to tell past from present. Perhaps the play should have been called *The Dying of a Salesman,* because Willy is dying throughout. That is the pathos of Linda's passionate injunction that attention must be finally paid to such a person, a human being to whom a terrible thing is happening. Nothing finds Willy anymore; everything loses him. He is a man upon whom the sun has gone down, to appropriate a great phrase from Ezra Pound. But have we defined as yet what is particular about his pathos?

I think not. Miller, a passionate moralist, all but rabbinical in his ethical vision, insists upon giving us Willy's, and his sons', sexual infidelities as synecdoches of the failure of Willy's vision of reality. Presumably, Willy's sense of failure, his belief that he has no right to his wife, despite Linda's love for him, is what motivates Willy's deceptions, and those of his sons after him. Yet Willy is not destroyed by his sense of failure. Miller may be a better interpreter of Miller than he is a dramatist. I find it wholly persuasive that Willy is destroyed by love, by his sudden awareness that his son Biff truly loves him. Miller beautifully comments that Willy resolves to die when "he is given his existence . . . his fatherhood, for which he has always striven and which until now he could not achieve." That evidently is the precise and terrible pathos of Willy's character and of his fate. He is a good man, who wants only to earn and to deserve the love of his wife and of his sons. He is self-slain, not by the salesman's dream of America, but by the universal desire to be loved by one's own, and to be loved beyond what one believes one deserves. Miller is not one of the masters of metaphor, but in *Death of a Salesman* he memorably achieves a pathos that none of us would be wise to dismiss.

RAYMOND WILLIAMS

Arthur Miller: An Overview

In the vigour of American life and speech, many elements of European drama found new variants and successes. Eugene O'Neill was directly inspired by Strindberg, but in *Anna Christie* and *Desire under the Elms* the significant element is the liveliness of the vernacular: a discovery of the resources of popular speech comparable in strength and intention to that of the Irish dramatists. O'Neill, in fact, had other and complicating dramatic purposes: the paradox of his work is his success in the vernacular and his increasing attachment to what is essentially isolated experience—a discovery or imposition of internally determined and abstract patterns (the success and failure of these modes is indicated in the analyses of *Mourning Becomes Electra* and *Long Day's Journey into Night*). In the 1920s, there was a vigorous American expressionist theatre, moving from O'Neill's *Emperor Jones* and *The Hairy Ape* to Elmer Rice's *The Adding Machine,* and in the 1930s there was a further lively experiment in radical dramatic forms, as in Odets's *Waiting for Lefty.*

This important and native experimental tradition is not easy to bring into focus with the contemporary European tradition in which many of the innovating forms had been discovered. It was perhaps only after 1945, and then from the cinema even more than the theatre, that the current of serious influence began to flow the other way. The major American dramatist remains Eugene O'Neill, but it was in Arthur Miller, in those post-war years, that the American tradition seemed most lively and fertile. While lacking

From *Drama: From Ibsen to Brecht.* © 1952 by Raymond Williams. Chatto & Windus, Ltd., 1952.

O'Neill's range, he was also easier to understand. The strange and restless genius of O'Neill was perhaps only clearly understood in the posthumous plays of the middle-late 1950s.

Meanwhile the work of Tennessee Williams was intensely influential in the theatre: following Strindberg and early O'Neill it remains a classic instance of the dramatization of intensely private and destructive passion; it is, in a literal sense, drama on a hot tin roof: the direct communication, to the nerves of an audience, of raw and essentially inarticulate experience: with the strengths of popular music and of an intensely personal kind of acting or acting-out; but with the dramatic design, often locally effective, revealing itself essentially as a highly professional theatrical contrivance. The line from *Lady Julie* to *Cat on a Hot Tin Roof* is obvious enough, in its strengths; but it represents also a domestication of that strangeness, a professional appropriation and exploitation of the methods of dramatic disturbance. It has of course in this respect been very widely imitated. There is now an effective sub-culture of just this kind of direct exposure of harsh and disintegrated feeling. In its strengths and weaknesses it seems to relate directly to an assenting structure of feeling in its audiences, and it is understandable that in this sense it has broken out of drama and the theatre and is finding, as it must find, less conventional and less independent forms: the completion of its own internal logic, which requires an assenting participation in a temporary accentuation and release of disturbance.

Arthur Miller, by comparison, is a traditional figure, but his works have an independence of occasion which contrasts very markedly with this alternative American tradition. His first two published plays—he had written seven or eight others before getting the recognition of production—were *All My Sons* (1947) and *Death of a Salesman* (1949). These show very well some of the problems of the post-war dramatist, in relating method to experience. For their themes, obviously, are very deeply linked, but their methods show a very marked contrast. *All My Sons* has been described as an Ibsenite play, and certainly, if we restrict Ibsen to the kind of play he wrote between *The League of Youth* (1869) and *Rosmersholm* (1886), it is a relevant description. The similarities are indeed so striking that we could call *All My Sons* pastiche if the force of its conception were not so evident. It is perhaps that much rarer case, of a writer who temporarily discovers in an existing form an exact way of realizing his own experience. At the centre of the play is the kind of situation which was Ibsen's development of the device of the "fatal secret." Joe Keller, a small manufacturer, has (in a similar way to Consul Bernick in *Pillars of Society*) committed a social crime for which he has escaped responsibility. He acquiesced in the sending of defective parts to the American Air Force in wartime, and yet allowed another man to take the consequences and imprisonment. The action begins after the war, and is basically on the lines of what has been called Ibsen's retrospective method (it was always much more than a device of exposition; it is a thematic forcing of past into present). The Ibsen method of showing first an ordinary domestic scene, into which, by gradual infiltration, the crime and the guilt enter and build up to the critical eruption, is exactly followed. The process of this destructive infiltration is carefully worked out in terms of the needs of the other characters—Keller's wife and surviving son, the girl the son is to marry, the neighbours, the son of the convict—so that the demonstration of social consequence, and therefore of Keller's guilt, is not of any abstract principle, but of personal needs and relationships, which compose a reality that directly enforces the truth. If Keller's son had not wanted to marry the convicted man's daughter (and they had been childhood friends; it was that neighbourhood which Keller's act disrupted); if his wife, partly in reaction to her knowledge of his guilt, had not maintained the superstition that their son killed in the war was still alive; if the action had been between strangers or business acquaintances, rather than between neighbours and neighbouring families, the truth would never have come out. Thus we see a true social reality, which includes both social relationships and absolute personal needs, enforcing a social fact—that of responsibility and consequence. This is still the method of Ibsen in the period named, and the device of climax—a concealed letter from Keller's dead son, who had known of his father's guilt—is again directly in Ibsen's terms.

The elements of theatrical contrivance in Ibsen's plays of this kind, and in *All My Sons,* are now sufficiently clear. Yet the total effect of such a play is undoubtedly powerful if its experience truly corresponds to its conventions. In historical terms, this is a bourgeois form, with that curious combination of a demonstrated public morality and an intervening fate, evident in the early eighteenth-century domestic drama, and reaching its maturity in Ibsen. To a considerable extent, *All My Sons* is a successful late example of this form, but a point is reached, in Miller's handling of the experience, where its limits are touched. For, as he rightly sees it, the social reality is more than a mechanism of honesty and right dealing, more than Ibsen's definition—

The spirits of Truth and Freedom, these are the pillars of society.

Miller reaches out to a deeper conception of relationships, which he emphasizes in his title. This is something more than honesty and uprightness; it is the quite different social conception of human brotherhood—

> I think to him they were all my sons. And I guess they were, I
> guess they were.

Moreover, Miller sees this in a social context, as he explains in the Introduction to his *Collected Plays:*

> Joe Keller's trouble . . . is not that he cannot tell right from
> wrong but that his cast of mind cannot admit that he, personally,
> has any viable connection with his world, his universe, or his
> society. He is not a partner in society, but an incorporated mem-
> ber, so to speak, and you cannot sue personally the officers of a
> corporation. I hasten to make clear that I am not merely speak-
> ing of a literal corporation but the concept of a man's becoming
> a function of production or distribution to the point where his
> personality becomes divorced from the actions it propels.

This concept, though Miller does not use the term, is the classical Marxist
concept of alienation, and it is with alienation both in a social action and in
a personality that Miller is ultimately concerned. The true social reality—
the needs and destinies of other persons—is meant to break down this
alienated consciousness, and restore the fact of consequence, of significant
and continuing relationships, in this man and in his society. But then it is at
this point that the limits of the form are damaging. The words I have
quoted, expressing Keller's realization of a different kind of consciousness,
have to stand on their own, because unlike the demonstration of ordinary
social responsibility they have no action to support them, and moreover as
words they are limited to the conversational resources so adequate elsewhere in the play, but wholly inadequate here to express so deep and
substantial a personal discovery (and if it is not this it is little more than a
maxim, a "sentiment"). It is at this point that we see the naturalist form—
even a principled naturalism, as in Ibsen and Miller and so rarely in others;
even this substantially and powerfully done—breaking down as it has so
often broken down, because the consciousness which the form was designed
to express is in any serious terms obsolete, and was already, by Miller
himself, being reached beyond.

There is an interesting account, in Miller's introduction, of the genesis
of *All My Sons,* relating it to a previous play and the discovery that

> two of the characters, who had been friends in the previous
> drafts, were logically brothers and had the same father. . . . The
> overt story was only tangential to the secret drama which its
> author was quite unconsciously trying to write. . . . In writing of

the father-son relationship and of the son's search for his relatedness there was a fullness of feeling I had never known before.
The crux of *All My Sons* was formed; and the roots of *Death of
a Salesman* were sprouted.

This is extremely important, not only as a clue to the plays named, but as
indicating the way in which Miller, personally, came to the experience
expressible as that of human brotherhood. In any sense that matters, this
concept is always personally known and lived; as a slogan it is nothing. And
the complicated experience of inheritance from a father is perhaps one of
the permanent approaches to this transforming consciousness. There is the
creative complexity of the fact that a son, in many senses, replaces his
father. There is dependence and the growth to independence, and both are
necessary, in a high and moving tension. In both father and son there are the
roots of guilt, and yet ultimately they stand together as men—the father
both a model and a rejected ideal; the son both an idea and a relative failure.
But the model, the rejection, the idea and the failure are all terms of growth,
and the balance that can be struck is a very deep understanding of relatedness and brotherhood. One way of looking at *All My Sons* is in these
universal terms: the father, in effect, destroys one of his sons, and that son,
in his turn, gives sentence of death on him, while at the same time, to the
other son, the father offers a future, and the son, in rejecting it, destroys his
father, in pain and love. Similarly, in *Death of a Salesman,* Willy Loman,
like Joe Keller, has lived for his sons, will die for the son who was to extend
his life, yet the sons, in their different ways, reject him, in one case for good
reasons, and in effect destroy him. Yet the failure on both sides is rooted in
love and dependence; the death and the love are deeply related aspects of the
same relationship. This complex, undoubtedly, is the "secret drama" of
which Miller writes, and if it is never wholly expressed it is clearly the real
source of the extraordinary dramatic energy.

    Death of a Salesman takes the moment of crisis in which Joe Keller
could only feebly express himself, and makes of it the action of the whole
play. Miller's first image was of

an enormous face . . . which would appear and then open up, we
would see the inside of a man's head. In fact, *The Inside of His
Head* was the first title.

This, in dramatic terms, is expressionism, and correspondingly the guilt of
Willy Loman is not in the same world as that of Joe Keller: it is not a single
act, subject to public process, needing complicated grouping and plotting to

make it emerge; it is, rather, the consciousness of a whole life. Thus the expressionist method, in the final form of the play, is not a casual experiment, but rooted in the experience. It is the drama of a single mind, and moreover,

> it would be false to a more integrated—or less disintegrating— personality.

It is historically true that expressionism is attuned to the experience of disintegration. In general dramatic history, as in Miller's own development, it arises at that point where the limits of naturalism are touched and a hitherto stable form begins to break. Yet *Death of a Salesman* is actually a development of expressionism, of an interesting kind. As Miller puts it:

> I had always been attracted and repelled by the brilliance of German expressionism after World War I, and one aim in *Salesman* was to employ its quite marvellous shorthand for humane "felt" characterisations rather than for purposes of demonstration for which the Germans had used it.

This is a fair comment on one aspect of, say, Toller, and the split of expressionism into "personal" and "social" kinds is related to an important general dissociation of contemporary experience. *Death of a Salesman* is an expressionist reconstruction of naturalist substance, and the result is not hybrid but a powerful particular form. The continuity from social expressionism remains clear, however, for I think in the end it is not Willy Loman as a man, but the image of the Salesman, that predominates. The social figure sums up the theme of alienation, for this is a man who from selling things has passed to selling himself, and has become, in effect, a commodity which like other commodities will at a certain point be economically discarded. The persuasive atmosphere of the play (which the slang embodies so perfectly, for it is a social result of this way of living) is one of false consciousness—the conditioned attitudes in which Loman trains his sons— being broken into by real consciousness, in actual life and relationships. The expressionist method embodies this false consciousness much more powerfully than naturalism could do. In *All My Sons* it had to rest on a particular crime, which could then be seen as in a limiting way personal—Keller the black sheep in a white flock—although the fundamental criticism was of a common way of living and thinking. The "marvellous shorthand" is perfectly adapted to exposing this kind of illusion and failure. At the same time the structure of personal relationships, within this method, must be seen as in a sense arbitrary; it has nothing of the rooted detail which the naturalism of *All My Sons* in this respect achieved. The golden football hero, the giggling woman in the hotel, the rich brother and similar figures seem to me to be clichés from the thinner world of a work like *Babbitt,* which at times the play uncomfortably resembles. The final figure of a man killing himself for the insurance money caps the whole process of the life that has been demonstrated, but "demonstrated," in spite of Miller's comment on the Germans, is the word that occurs to one to describe it. The emotional power of the demonstration is considerable, and is markedly increased by the brilliant expressionist staging. Yet, by the high standards which Miller insists on, and in terms of the essential realism to which he seems to be reaching, the contrast of success and failure within both *All My Sons* and *Death of a Salesman* points finally to the radical and still unsolved difficulties of form.

The Crucible (1952) is a powerful and successful dramatization of the notorious witch trials of Salem, but it is technically less interesting than its predecessors just because it is based on a historical event which at the level of action and principled statement is explicit enough to solve, or not to raise, the difficult dramatic problems which Miller had previously set himself. The importance of the witch trials is that in them, in a clear and exciting way, the moral crisis of a society is explicit, is directly enacted and stated, in such a way that the quality of the whole way of life is organically present and evident in the qualities of persons. Through this action Miller brilliantly expresses a particular crisis—the modern witch hunt—in his own society, but it is not often, in our own world, that the issues and statements so clearly emerge in a naturally dramatic form. The methods explored in the earlier plays are not necessary here, but the problems they offered to solve return immediately, outside the context of this particular historical event. *The Crucible* is a fine play, but it is also a quite special case.

In *A Memory of Two Mondays* (1955), Miller returns to the direct dramatization of modern living, and as if to underline the point made about *The Crucible* (of which, as the introduction shows, he was completely aware) seeks to make a new form out of the very facts of inconsequence, discontinuity and the deep frustrations of inarticulacy, which is at once a failure of speech and the wider inability of men to express themselves in certain kinds of work and working relationship. Instead of concentrating these themes in a particular history, pointed by plot or single crisis, he deploys them in the scattered form of a series of impressions, with the dramatic centre in memory rather than in action or crisis. The work atmosphere is in some ways significantly caught, and there is always the mark of Miller's insight into the importance and passion of what many others dismiss as "ordinary" lives.

There is an occasional flare of dramatic feeling, as in the last speech of Gus, but in general the tension is much lower than in the earlier plays, and the dramatic methods seem often mere devices. The Irish singer and reciter; the insets of flat sub-Auden verse; the lighting and scenic devices of the passing of time: these, at this tension, seem mechanical. And a central image of the play—when the workers clean the windows to let in a sight of sun and trees, and let in actually a view of a cat-house (brothel)—seems contrived. Miller's fertility of experiment is important, but experiment, as here, involves failure.

A View from the Bridge (1955; revised 1957) brings back the intensity. The capacity to touch and stir deep human feeling was marked in the earlier plays, but Miller has said, interestingly, (it is his essential difference from Tennessee Williams, with whom he is often linked):

> The end of drama is the creation of a higher consciousness and not merely a subjective attack upon the audience's nerves and feelings.

The material of A View from the Bridge is to most people deeply disturbing, and Miller's first impulse was to keep it abstract and distant, to hold back

> the empathic flood which a realistic portrayal of the same tale and characters might unloose.

But, in his own view, he went too far in this direction, and subsequently revised the play towards a more intense realism. The distancing element remains, however, in the use of a commentator, or raisonneur, and, though there are false notes in the writing of this part, it is an important reason for the play's success.

A View from the Bridge follows from the earlier works in that it shows a man being broken and destroyed by guilt. Its emphasis is personal, though the crisis is related to the intense primary relationships of an insecure and partly illegal group—a Brooklyn waterfront slum, with ties back to Italy, receiving unauthorized immigrants and hiding them within its own fierce loyalties. Eddie Carbone's breakdown is sexual, and the guilt, as earlier, is deeply related to love. And the personal breakdown leads to a sin against this community, when in the terror of his complicated jealousies Eddie betrays immigrants of his wife's kin to the external law.

At the centre of the drama again is the form of a relationship between parent and child, but here essentially displaced so that the vital relationship is between a man and the niece to whom he has been as a father. The girl's coming to adolescence provokes a crisis which is no more soluble than if they had really been father and child, yet to a degree perhaps is more admissible into consciousness. Eddie is shown being destroyed by forces which he cannot control, and the complex of love and guilt has the effect of literal disintegration, in that the known sexual rhythms break down into their perverse variations: the rejection of his wife, as his vital energy transfers to the girl, and then the shattering crisis in which within the same rush of feeling he moves into the demonstration of both incestuous and homosexual desires. The crisis burns out his directions and meanings, and he provokes his death shouting, "I want my name." This establishment of significance, after breakdown, through death, was the pattern of Joe Keller and Willy Loman; of John Proctor, in heroic stance, in *The Crucible;* of Gus, in a minor key, in *A Memory of Two Mondays.* We are at the heart, here, of Miller's dramatic pattern, and his work, in this precise sense, is tragedy—the loss of meaning in life turns to the struggle for meaning by death. The loss of meaning is always a personal history, though in Willy Loman it comes near to being generalized. Equally, it is always set in the context of a loss of social meaning, a loss of meaning in relationships. The point is made, and is ratifying, in the commentary in *A View from the Bridge:*

> Now we are quite civilized, quite American. Now we settle for half.

and again, at the end:

> Something perversely pure calls to me from his memory—not purely good, but himself purely, for he allowed himself to be wholly known and for that I think I will love him more than all my sensible clients. And yet, it is better to settle for half, it must be! And so I mourn him—I admit it—with a certain alarm.

Tempted always to settle for half—for the loss of meaning and the loss of consequence endemic in the whole complex of personal and social relationships, the American way of living as Miller sees it—the heroes of these plays, because, however perversely, they are still attached to life, still moved by irresistible desires for a name, a significance, a vital meaning, break out and destroy themselves, leaving their own comment on the half-life they have experienced. It is a powerful and connecting action.

Yet its dramatic problems remained considerable, and were illustrated, retrospectively, by Miller's most confused play, *After the Fall,* which appeared in 1964. This was said to be intensely autobiographical, but the more important point is that, under the tension reached in *A View from the*

Bridge—between a virtually uncontrollable guilt and confusion, and a way of seeing just these experiences in a communicable pattern of relationships—Miller moved, in effect, to the alternative tradition: the direct exposure of inarticulate private feeling, and beyond this the essentially abstract imposition of a pattern of universal guilt. This pattern is strictly suggestive: an incoherent phrasing and gesturing of a metaphysical meaning—the separateness of every human being, the inevitability of betrayal, the reduction of social guilt to a common but incommunicable private neurosis. What had been dramatically present in the earlier plays—an undogmatic, substantial point of view towards the action, which sustained a consciousness other than the take-it-or-leave-it confession of disturbance—is now absent; what replaces it is a confusion between the main actor and the narration, which is then itself at the level of the disturbed and suggestive confession. It is very significant, historically, that Miller should have moved to this alternative method, which has the weight and disturbance of a culture behind it:

> QUENTIN: Murder?
> *(His mother stumbles into darkness, her hands in prayer, whispering "I will die, I will die." He turns to Maggie who is now getting to her hands and knees, gasping. He rushes to help her, terrified by his realization, but she flails out at him, and on one elbow looks up at him in a caricature of laughter, her eyes victorious and wild with fear.)*
> MAGGIE: Now we both know. You tried to kill me, mister. I been killed by a lot of people, some couldn't hardly spell, but it's the same, mister. You're on the end of a long, long line.

It is hardly any longer dramatic writing. It is the notation of a different convention: the alternative tradition of semi-articulate exposure. It cannot be taken as an epilogue to Miller, and it does not cancel his earlier work, but it shows both the difficulties of development of the form he had chosen and the intense disintegrating pressures of a powerful contemporary structure of feeling.

TOM F. DRIVER

Strength and Weakness in Arthur Miller

Arthur Miller's introduction to his *Collected Plays* (New York, 1957) is one of the major documents of American theatre. It reveals an eminent playwright having struggled to understand and perfect his craft. It shows him eager to use the theatre to express his evolving ideas. It shows his strengths, and also his weaknesses.

The foremost asset Arthur Miller possesses as a playwright is his knowledge that the theatre must dedicate itself to public matters. He has an acute sense of his audience as persons to be addressed, never merely spectators to be tolerated. "A play," he writes, "ought to make sense to common-sense people . . . the only challenge worth the effort is the widest one and the tallest one, which is the people themselves."

His writing, although it usually has an axe to grind, does not attempt to startle society with new ideas. Indeed, he does not believe that the theatre *can* promulgate entirely new ideas, because it must gather the assent of its audience as it moves along, and this is impossible with the radically new. The theatre should enunciate "not-yet-popular ideas which are already in the air, ideas for which there has already been a preparation by non-dramatic media." Thus he understands the vigor of theatrical art to depend in part on its timeliness: drama is "the art of the present tense par excellence." It follows that the theatre binds isolated human beings into their essential corporateness: "I regard the theatre as a serious business, one that makes or should make man more human, which is to say, less alone."

From *Tulane Drama Review* 4, no. 4 (May 1960). © 1960 by the *Tulane Drama Review*.

A corollary of this "public" view of theatre is the belief that psychology is an insufficient basis for it. Psychology becomes preoccupied with the individual, in many cases even the idiosyncratic, whereas the proper concerns of the theatre are social. Miller says that he himself has "shown a preference for plays which seek causation not only in psychology but in society."

If one takes the "public" view of theatre seriously, he will be forced to ponder the nature of dramatic action and, with it, the importance of the handling of time in the structuring of a play. It has often been said that the problem of dramatic construction is the problem of handling exposition, a truism Miller repeats when he writes, in discussing Ibsen, that "the biggest single dramatic problem" is "how to dramatize what has gone before." It is something other than a truism, however, when he adds:

> I say this not merely out of technical interest, but because dramatic characters, and the drama itself, can never hope to attain a maximum degree of consciousness unless they contain a viable unveiling of the contrast between past and present, and an awareness of the process by which the present has become what it is.

Miller rightly perceives that one of Ibsen's greatest strengths lay in his ability to manage theatrical time so as to express the sequence of causation which he saw in the lives of the characters in his plays. Miller also sees that re-arrangement of time-sequences is tantamount to a change in the implied causal relationships between events. It was just because the notion of causation was so different in *All My Sons* from what it came to be in *Death of a Salesman* that the former remained an "old fashioned" play of exposition, confrontation, and climax, whereas the latter involved "an explosion of watch and calendar," with a corresponding change in the level of reality to which it appealed.

It is hardly possible to read Miller without being impressed with his desire to see and report life realistically. He tells us that when he was writing *A Memory of Two Mondays*, he desired "to be abrupt, clear, and explicit in setting forth fact as fact and art as art so that the sea of theatrical sentiment, which is so easily let in to drown all shape, meaning, and perspective, might be held back and some hard outline of a human dilemma be allowed to rise and stand." Even though there is melodrama in *All My Sons, The Crucible*, and *A View from the Bridge*, it is difficult to reflect on Miller's work without feeling that a hard realism is informing most, if not all, of his concrete observations.

It is the more to his credit as a thinker that his notion of the real is not limited by the canons of what has come to be known in the theatre as "realism." He is quite aware that multiple meanings are attached to the word "real," and while his bent of mind seems to prevent him from investigating the concept of "the real" philosophically, he is far from assuming that the only reality is the positive concrete:

> The longer I dwelt on the whole spectacle, [human dedication to evil] the more clear became the failure of the present age to find a universal moral sanction, and the power of realism's hold on our theatre was an aspect of this vacuum. For it began to appear that our inability to break more than the surfaces of realism reflected our inability—playwrights and audiences—to agree upon the pantheon of forces and values which must lie behind the realistic surfaces of life. In this light, realism, as a style, could seem to be a defense against the assertion of meaning. How strange a conclusion this is when one realizes that the same style seventy years ago was the prime instrument of those who sought to illuminate meaning in the theatre.

Miller describes the way his research into the Salem witch-trials led him to understand the limited frame of reference in which modern realistic discourse must be carried on. Out of this came his subsequent attempt to go beyond limitations of realistic theatre. It is an enlightening tale of a pragmatic mind's discovery of the usefulness of religious language.

What Miller asks for is a theatre of "heightened consciousness." He speaks of two passions in man, the "passion to feel" and the "passion to know." It is his conviction that we need, and can have, more of the latter. "Drama is akin to the other inventions of man in that it ought to help us to know more, and not merely to spend our feelings." The experience of writing *The Crucible* seems to have shown him that a theatre given more to objective knowledge, to heightened self-awareness, is possible. He mentions Brecht as one who has tackled the central problem of contemporary drama, "which is again the problem of consciousness." And in speaking of *Death of a Salesman,* he has the courage to mention its chief limitation when he asks, "but was there not another realm even higher, where feeling took awareness more openly by the hand and both equally ruled and were illuminated?"

These, then, are the strengths of Arthur Miller: an acute awareness of the "public" nature of theatre, the desire to see and report life realistically, an unwillingness to settle for a merely positivist version of reality, and a desire to see a theatre of "heightened consciousness." By putting these concerns before the public, Arthur Miller has shown that his sights are higher than those of any of his competitors at the Broadway box-office. The fact that such concerns exist in a playwright of his prominence is proof that our theatre is still alive.

It is perhaps unfair to judge Miller's work as a playwright by his own critical standard. To do so, however, will reveal not only the deficiencies of much American theatre but will also be a way of seeing certain weaknesses that lie in Miller's thought.

We must remember that the only success both popular and critical Miller has had in this country is *Death of a Salesman*. We must also re-member that it remains more consistently upon the level of psychology and feeling than do any of his other plays. The original title for it was *The Inside of His Head,* and the objective, apparently, was to create a dramatic form which "would literally be the process of Willy Loman's way of mind." The result was the kind of play, says Miller, which "issues in a genuine poetry of feeling," and in which feeling is "raised up as the highest good and the ultimate attainment in drama."

It was beyond this level that he wished to go in achieving that other realm, "where feeling took awareness more openly by the hand." Yet when he attempted that other realm in *The Crucible* and *A View from the Bridge,* he was not successful. After *A View from the Bridge* failed in New York, it was revised and later played successfully in London; but it is instructive to note that the revisions were all in the direction of making the psychology of the central character more prominent. Indeed, it had been obvious all along that, although the author of *A View from the Bridge* had wanted to write a play in which action took precedence over psychology, he had chosen for this purpose a character and situation bound to interest the audience pri-marily from a psychological point of view. It was the story of a Brooklyn longshoreman unconsciously in love with his niece, a man who destroys all his family because of jealousy.

In classical times, such a theme might have served a transpsychological purpose; but in Miller's play there was no level of meaning, law, provi-dence, or fate, upon which an action that transcended character might rest. The action inevitably fell back, as it were, into the subjectivity of Eddie and his uncontrollable jealousy. No genuine parallel with the Greek drama had been found. In the case of Oedipus, for instance, the objective realm is clearly expressed in the problem of the health of the Theban *polis,* the proscriptions against patricide and incest, and the search for truth as a self-evident good. Nothing on this level was present in *A View from the*

Bridge, yet without it no theatre of action rather than character is possible. Mr. Miller had not, in short, solved the problem of "the failure of the present age to find a universal moral sanction," and without such a solution, in one degree or another, there was nothing other than psychology to support the action of his play.

From this experience Mr. Walter Kerr would doubtless argue, as he does in *How Not to Write a Play,* that it is only psychological consistency and the creation of interesting character which makes good plays, and that the one undoubted success of Arthur Miller, *Death of a Salesman,* shows it. All that it really shows, however, is that Arthur Miller is typical of our theatre in being able to do character best and in not being able to sustain a more comprehensive kind of action.

Two weaknesses are fatal to Miller's attempt to write the kind of objective theatre he sees is needed. First, his view of man in society is too narrow. He is restricted, as many have pointed out, by a particular social theory which he seems not to have had the inclination to probe until it yielded him a fundamental idea of human nature. Brecht, to take an opposite example, did such probing. Apparently Miller's Marxism changes as he goes along, and it would be going beyond the evidence to suggest that he adheres to any "line," whether political or ideological. Nevertheless, he bears a quasi-Marxist stamp and most of his plays tend to become mere partisan social critique. The momentary usefulness of that social critique, or the extent to which it actually is Marxist, is nothing to the point. The point is simply that his conception of the "reality" with which man must deal is limited.

Miller has some lofty things to say about *All My Sons* being an attack upon "unrelatedness" and about crime "having roots in a certain relationship of the individual to society"; but when all is said and done, the play seems to be only a play about an aircraft-parts manufacturer in wartime. It has rapidly become dated. The mistake was not in being timely, but in being timely with too simple a point of view. *The Crucible* invited the immediate application to the McCarthy issue which it received, and which made it seem small. When it was revived in 1958 off Broadway, it did have more success than in its first run during the McCarthy era. Even then, however, I found the play strident, written with an emotion inappropriate to its inner life.

Our drama is condemned, so to speak, to the emotions of subjectivism, which, as they approach knowledge and self-awareness, become less and less actual and real to us. In retrospect, I think that my course in *The Crucible* should have been toward greater self-awareness and not, as my critics have implied, toward an enlarged and more pervasive subjectivism.

The goal is right. It is not reached because Miller's sense of objectivity is not comprehensive enough. He lacks that metaphysical inquisitiveness which would take him to the bottom of the problems he encounters. One might say that he sees the issues too soon, sees them in their preliminary form of social or even moral debate, but not in terms of dramatic events that disturb the audience's idea of basic truth, which is the foundation for its moral attitudes. It is the genius of a Pirandello, a Brecht, or an Ionesco to cause such disturbance and by doing so to become genuine moral critics. Miller's limited theatre fits down inside the theatre of the world which the audience inhabits. His theatre is too small to touch the outer walls against which the genuinely objective drama would need to be played.

This point is made very clear in certain remarks he makes about *Death of a Salesman,* especially as we compare them with the confusion which lurks in every corner of that play. The following passage occurs in a discussion of Willy Loman's stature as a tragic figure:

> How can we respect a man who goes to such extremities over something he could in no way help or prevent? The answer, I think, is not that we respect the man, but that we respect the Law he has so completely broken, wittingly or not, for it is that Law which, we believe, defines us as men. The confusion of some critics viewing *Death of a Salesman* in this regard is that they do not see that Willy Loman has broken a law without whose protection life is insupportable if not incomprehensible to him and to many others; it is the law which says that a failure in society and in business has no right to live. Unlike the law against incest, the law of success is not administered by statute of church, but it is very nearly as powerful in its grip upon men. The confusion increases because, while it is a law, it is by no means a wholly agreeable one even as it is slavishly obeyed, for to fail is no longer to belong to society, in his estimate.

The confusion, I am afraid, lies not with the critics but with the playwright, and it is a very illustrative one. There is, in fact, no "law which says that a failure in society and in business has no right to live." It would, indeed, suit Miller's polemic better if there were. There is a *delusion* that a failure in society and in business has no right to live. To some people, such as Willy Loman, it may indeed seem like a law. But it is one thing for a character in a play to act as if something were a law, and quite another thing for the playwright to believe it. Miller's subsequent remarks in this same section of his essay make it perfectly clear that he himself, the audience, and also Willy Loman, do as a matter of fact have criteria according to which they suspect that this "law" is a hoax. It is in fact not a law but a false *credo*, which Willy shares with many persons, and the result of the attempt to make a false *credo* into a law results only in pathetic irony.

What is it, one wonders, that prevents Miller from probing Willy's consciousness and ours to the point of finding the truly objective world in which we still, in fact, believe and according to which Willy's "law" strikes us as so pathetic? If we ask where in the play one touches bedrock, the answer is nowhere. Is the law of success *really* a law? No. Miller tells us that "the system of love," which is "embodied in Biff Loman" was meant to counter Willy's "law." But if that is true, it was unfortunately not dramatized. That is, the way in which Biff's "law" of love judges and invalidates Willy's "law" of success is not revealed, and so the one is not actually a truth which is being brought to bear dramatically on the other.

The same ambiguity is seen in the question of society versus the individual. John Gassner said long ago that Arthur Miller had "split his play between *social causation* and *individual responsibility* for Willy's fate." Is Willy's "law" the result of some defect in himself? If so, what is the nature of this defect, and what genuine law does it confound? Or is his "law" imposed upon him by a white-collar industrial society? If so, what is wrong with such a society and what truth does it prevent Willy Loman from seeing? Miller would probably resist making a decision in favor of either the individual or the social causation, and rightly so. But in that case, if he is interested in theatre worth the name of art, he has an obligation to examine his complex situation until the roots of Willy's anxiety are exposed, an exposure which would cause us to know something about the reality in which we are, if only unconsciously, living. It is in the lack of penetration into the objective philosophical situation that Miller fails us, with the result that we must settle for no more enlightenment upon our situation than pathetic Willy had upon his.

Miller deplores the loss of a "universal moral sanction," but he does nothing toward the discovery of a conceivable basis for one. In that respect he is, perhaps, no different from the majority of his contemporaries. It is not a surprising result, however, that he falls so easily into preaching and scolding his audience. (In his essay in the *Collected Plays* he is not above reproving those who staged or acted his plays, an attitude which reflects credit upon no one, least of all the playwright.) Miller's strident moralism is a good example of what happens when ideals must be maintained in an atmosphere of humanistic relativism. There being no objective good and evil, and no imperative other than conscience, man himself must be made to bear the full burden of creating his values and living up to them. The immensity of this task is beyond human capacity, even that of genius. To insist upon it without reference to ultimate truth is to create a situation productive of despair. This point has been seen by many writers of our day, but not by the liberal optimists, of which Miller is one. Here we have come to the second weakness which inevitably robs his work of stature.

At the time that *The Crucible* opened, Eric Bentley categorized Arthur Miller as an unreconstructed liberal and said that he "is the playwright of American liberal folklore." The trouble with the play, he went on, was that it too neatly divided the sheep from the goats. "The guilty men are as black with guilt as Mr. Miller says—what we must ask is whether the innocent are as white with innocence." Mr. Bentley's remarks become all the more interesting when they are remembered in connection with a passage in the Introduction to the *Collected Plays,* in which Miller describes his discovery, while writing *The Crucible,* of certain facts about human nature:

> I believe now, as I did not conceive then, that there are people dedicated to evil in the world; that without their perverse example we should not know the good. Evil is not a mistake but a fact in itself . . . I believe merely that, from whatever cause, a dedication to evil, not mistaking it for good, but knowing it as evil and loving it as evil, is possible in human beings who appear agreeable and normal. I think now that one of the hidden weaknesses of our whole approach to dramatic psychology is our inability to face this fact—to conceive, in effect, of Iago.

So far, we are on fairly safe ground, although we must note already that only certain people are dedicated to evil, others presumably going clean. But note how contradictory are the following sentiments. They are from the very same passage, in the place indicated above by the ellipsis:

> I have never proceeded psychoanalytically in my thought, but neither have I been separated from that humane if not humanistic conception of man as being essentially innocent while the evil in him represents but a perversion of his frustrated love. I posit no metaphysical force of evil which totally possesses certain individuals, nor do I even deny that given infinite wisdom and pa-

tience and knowledge any human being can be saved from himself.

Here the contradictory and self-limiting sentiments pass clearly before us. Evil is a fact, yet it is only a perversion of frustrated love. It is as absolute as in Iago, yet it may be cured with wisdom, patience, and knowledge. It is outside one's self and may be loved, yet it is only from himself that man needs to be saved. The passage reveals a head-on collision between illusions of human goodness and the facts of dedication to evil. Here we reach the straits through which the Miller realism will not pass.

No wonder *Death of a Salesman* cannot make up its mind whether the trouble is in Willy or in society. No wonder Willy is at one moment the pathetic object of our pity and the next is being defended as a hero of tragic dimensions. Miller is a playwright who wants morality without bothering to speak of a good in the light of which morality would make sense. On the one hand he wants a universal moral sanction; on the other he considers man's potentialities and limitations to lie entirely within himself. Out of such unresolved contradictions irony and pathos are the most we can get, and we are lucky to get those.

The concluding sentence of the essay we have been considering reads as follows:

> If there is one unseen goal toward which every play in this book strives, it is that very discovery and its proof—that we are made and yet are more than what made us.

I take this to mean that man transcends his hereditary and environmental situation. Well and good. But if we are to be able to speak of "moral sanctions" in drama or society, we must come to acknowledge that man is himself transcended by some truth that is not irrelevant to morality. Miller seems to flinch before that assertive act of the imagination which uncovers (or, in religious language, receives) the ontological ground upon which the truly meaningful act must stand. This is a level of the real which Miller has not yet explored, although it is the level demanded of one who would break out of the confusions that enveloped Willy Loman.

ESTHER MERLE JACKSON

Death of a Salesman: *Tragic Myth in the Modern Theatre*

Perhaps the dominant theme in the drama of the twentieth century is an attempt to recover—or, more precisely, to restate—a tragic apprehension about the human condition. A pervasive concern about the ultimate meaning of human suffering is reflected, in one way or another, in the work of all of the major playwrights of the twentieth century: in that of Ibsen, Strindberg, Chekhov, Shaw, Claudel, Synge, Lorca, and O'Neill, as well as in that of Pirandello, Brecht, Sartre, Camus, and more recently, Wilder, Williams, Beckett, Genet, Albee, and others.

The American drama has been particularly concerned with the modern face of suffering. Since its emergence, barely a half-century ago, the American drama has attempted, rather consistently, to record the kinds of crises which have characterized our times. The great American masterworks—*Mourning Becomes Electra, The Time of Your Life, The Skin of Our Teeth, A Streetcar Named Desire,* and others—have been concerned with the response of mankind to rapid technological advance. But the American dramatist has encountered serious difficulties in his search for a mode of expression appropriate to this theme. For he has been handicapped by a critical problem affecting communication: by the absence of a body of natural myths—symbolic interpretations of the life of man. Unlike Aeschylus, Shakespeare, Corneille, or subsequent playwrights in the interrelated European traditions, the American dramatist has been unable to employ as the

From *College Language Association Journal* 7, no. 1 (September 1963). © 1963 by College Language Association.

instrumentation of his vision the great natural legends which are the residue of centuries of civilized growth.

The absence of conventional patterns of mythic interpretation has made it necessary for the American dramatist to devise new ways of seeing, interpreting, and re-creating reality. In terms of his ability to formulate coherent mythic patterns, perhaps the most effective dramatist in the American group is the "middle" playwright Arthur Miller. In his major works, *All My Sons, Death of a Salesman, The Crucible,* and *A View from the Bridge,* Miller seems to demonstrate a superiority to other American dramatists in the symbolic interpretation of universal dimensions of collective experience. Indeed, perhaps the most nearly mature myth about human suffering in an industrial age is Miller's masterwork, *Death of a Salesman.* In this work, first performed some thirteen years ago, Miller has formulated a statement about the nature of human crises in the twentieth century which seems, increasingly, to be applicable to the entire fabric of civilized experience. The superiority of *Death of a Salesman* over other worthy American dramas such as *Mourning Becomes Electra, A Streetcar Named Desire,* or Miller's own work, *The Crucible,* is the sensitivity of its myth: the critical relationship of its central symbol—the Salesman—to the interpretation of the whole of contemporary life. In this image, Miller brings into the theatre a figure who is, in our age, a kind of hero—a ritual representative of an industrial society. It is its intimate association with our aspirations which gives to the story of Loman an ambiguous, but highly affecting, substratum of religious, philosophical, political, and social meanings. The appearance of the Salesman Loman as the subject of moral exploration stirs the modern spectator at that alternately joyful and painful periphery of consciousness which is the province of tragedy. The enactment of his suffering, fall, and partial enlightenment, provokes a mixed response: that anger and delight, indignation and sympathy, pity and fear, which Aristotle described as "catharsis."

Miller writes that, in Loman, he has attempted to personify certain values which civilized men, in the twentieth century, share. The movement of tragedy from the ground of the lawless Titan Prometheus to that of the common man Loman does not represent, for Miller, a decline in values; on the contrary, it is evidence of a hopeful development. For Loman, a descendant of the nineteenth-century protagonists of Ibsen, Chekhov, Shaw, and others, reflects Western civilization's increasing concern with a democratic interpretation of moral responsibilities. *Death of a Salesman* attempts to explore the implications of a life for which men—not gods—are wholly responsible.

Some of the problems with the interpretation of this play have grown out of the author's own statements about his intent; that is to say, Miller seems to have created in *Death of a Salesman* a new form which transcended his conscious motive. *Death of a Salesman,* despite the presence of those social implications which Miller notes in his later essays, is a myth, not a document; that is to say, it is not, in the conventional sense, a problem play. Unlike Miller's earlier work, *All My Sons, Death of a Salesman* is not concerned with such human failings as may find permanent social, political, or even psychological remedy. *Death of a Salesman,* like *The Crucible* and *A View from the Bridge,* is, rather, a study of a man's existence in a metaphysical universe. It is, like *Agamemnon, Oedipus the King, Hamlet,* and *King Lear,* a mythic apprehension of life. Willy Loman, like the traditional tragic protagonist, symbolizes the cruel paradox of human existence. His story [according to Miller's introduction to *Collected Plays,*] stripped to its mythic essentials, is familiar:

> An aged king—a pious man—moves toward life's end. Instead of reaping the benefits of his piety, he finds himself caught in bewildering circumstances. Because of a mistake—an error in judgment—a tragic reversal has taken place in his life. Where he has been priest, knower of secrets, wielder of power, and symbol of life, he now finds himself adjudged defiler, usurper, destroyer, and necessary sacrifice. Like the traditional hero, Loman begins his long season of agony. In his descent, however, there is the familiar tragic paradox; for as he moves toward inevitable destruction, he acquires that knowledge, that sense of reconciliation, which allows him to conceive a redemptive plan for his house.

As in traditional tragedy, Loman—the ritual head of his house—seeks to discover a design in the paradoxical movement of life; to impose upon it a sense of meaning greater than that conferred upon it by actuality. The play asks the ancient questions: What real value is there in life? What evil resides in seeming good? What good is hidden in seeming evil? What permanence is buried beneath the face of change? What use can man make of his suffering?

Miller [in his introduction to *Collected Plays*] describes this drama as a study of the circumstances which affect human destiny in the moral universe:

> I take it that if one could know enough about a human being one could discover some conflict, some value, some challenge, how-

ever minor or major, which he cannot find it in himself to walk away from or turn his back on. The structure of these plays, in this respect, is to the end that such a conflict be discovered and clarified. Idea, in these plays, is the generalized meaning of that discovery applied to men other than the hero. Time, characterizations, and other elements are treated differently from play to play, but all to the end that that moment of commitment be brought forth, that moment when, in my eyes, a man differentiates himself from every other man, that moment when out of a sky full of stars he fixes on one star. I take it, as well, that the less capable a man is of walking away from the central conflict of the play, the closer he approaches a tragic existence. In turn, this implies that the closer a man approaches tragedy the more intense is his concentration of emotion upon the fixed point of his commitment. . . . The assumption—or presumption—behind these plays is that life has meaning.

Now the significant element in this statement is the playwright's suggestion that the ordinary actions of common men have ultimate meaning; indeed, that they are the concrete expression of conflict in the moral universe. The implication of this proposition is indeed profound. For it assigns primary responsibility for the conduct of the universe to man. Miller's position is, thus, opposed to that commonly assigned to Ibsen. Certainly, it is in contradiction to *Realism,* which is concerned primarily with the meaning of action and being in a material world. It is, similarly, at variance with the philosophy posited by so-called Christian dramatists such as Claudel and Thornton Wilder, who assign the larger role in the conduct of the universe to a divine power. Miller's position is, at this point, Sophoclean in nature. For like Sophocles, he suggests that the critical role in the moral universe is that of man himself.

Now Miller's classic stance is not singular in modern theatre. A study of the masterpieces of the last fifty years, both in Europe and in America, shows this classic concept of human responsibility to be common to many examples of contemporary drama. Miller's position is roughly parallel to that of Jean-Paul Sartre, who in an earlier discussion of contemporary French theatre, wrote:

For them [the young playwrights] the theatre will be able to present man in his entirety only in proportion to the theatre's willingness to be *moral.* By that we do not mean that it should put forward examples illustrating the rules of deportment or the practical ethics taught to children, but rather that the study of the conflict of characters should be replaced by the presentation of the conflict of rights . . . In each case, it is, in the final analysis and in spite of divergent interests, the systems of values, of ethics and of concepts of man which are lined up against each other . . . This theatre does not give its support to any one "thesis" and its not inspired by any preconceived idea. All it seeks to do is to explore the state of man in its entirety, and to present to the modern man a portrait of himself, his problems, his hopes and struggles.

Throughout the critical writings of the contemporaries, in the essays of O'Neill, Saroyan, Wilder, Williams, and Miller, as well as in the work of Europeans such as Sartre, Camus, Anouilh, and others, this dramatic motive is articulated: to illumine the moral choice which lies hidden beneath the face of actuality, to show modern man the present image of human destiny.

Now to say that Miller and others are in process of evolving a contemporary tragic myth is not to suggest that *Death of a Salesman* is an imitation of the Greek tragic form. Indeed, Miller states quite clearly [in his introduction to *Collected Plays*] that changes in the perception of universal law, as well as alterations in the very idea of man, would make Greek tragedy invalid as an expression of our time. He writes that he seeks, rather, to evolve a form which may stand in the same kind of relationship to the moral crises of the twentieth century as did Greek, Shakespearean, or French tragic drama—each to its own epoch. While Miller and others appear, then, to have adopted certain characteristics belonging to traditional tragedy, they have rejected others. *Death of a Salesman* appears to imitate classic tragedy primarily in its acceptance of the principle of the ultimate responsibility of the individual. That which appears to differentiate this work from traditional forms is its relocation of the tragic environment. For *Death of a Salesman,* like other examples of the contemporary *genre,* elevates to meaning a new protagonist: the common man. Perhaps of greater importance is the fact that it removes the ground of the tragic conflict from outer event to inner consciousness. *Death of a Salesman,* like *Mourning Becomes Electra, The Hairy Ape, A Streetcar Named Desire,* and others, may be described as a *tragedy of consciousness,* the imitation of a moral crisis in the life of a common man.

II

Miller [in his introduction to *Collected Plays*] traces this idea, in part, to the German expressionists, particularly, to Bertolt Brecht. Professor John Gassner finds aspects of this "underground drama" in the nineteenth-century innovators, not only in the work of the playwrights, Ibsen, Strindberg, Chekhov, and Shaw, but also in that of stream-of-consciousness novelists such as Dostoevsky, Tolstoy, and Henry James. But while the contemporary dramatists are indebted to these sources, the idea of form as the *imitation of consciousness* is much older than the late nineteenth century. Clearly, Miller and others have borrowed heavily from Shakespeare and his antecedents in the liturgical drama; moreover, their interpretations of the internal struggle have some of their roots in both classic and neoclassic tragedy.

The concept of tragedy as a crisis within the consciousness appears to have emerged clearly in the romantic period, particularly in the Sturm und Drang movement; in the theatre of Goethe, Schiller, Coleridge, Wagner, and Nietzsche. Oddly enough, the idea continued to dominate the theatre of the so-called "realists." It gained a systematic dramaturgy in expressionism; it has, throughout this century, intensified its hold upon the contemporary imagination. We may, thus, read the history of western drama—classicism, neoclassicism, romanticism, realism, and expressionism—as a continuous development; the gradual narrowing of theatrical focus upon the moment of crisis within the individual consciousness.

The adoption of this concept by modern dramatists has accounted for major alterations in form. The new form is not a representation of ordinary modes of action, an imitation of events-in-themselves. It is, rather, concerned with the representation of consciousness, with the imitation of a single moment of experience. We may describe *Death of a Salesman,* for example, as a kind of theatrical illusion. For it is intended, according to Miller [in his introduction to *Collected Plays*], as the apparition of a key image, the imitation of the "way of mind" which characterizes the Salesman Willy:

> The first image that occurred to me which was to result in *Death of a Salesman* was of an enormous face the height of the proscenium arch which would appear and then open up, and we would see the inside of a man's head . . . The *Salesman* image was from the beginning absorbed with the concept that nothing in life comes "next" but that everything exists together and at the same time within us; that there is no past to be "brought forward" in a human being, but that he is his past at every

moment and that the present is merely that which his past is capable of noticing and smelling and reacting to.

I wished to create a form which, in itself as a form, would literally be the process of Willy Loman's way of mind.

Death of a Salesman, as vision, follows an aesthetic, rather than a logical, mode of development. For it represents the protagonist's attempt to reconstitute the progression of his experience. Loman, as the protagonist, has an extremely complicated identity; for he is actor—observer-creator. He is the very ground of reality—the shape of experience itself; at the same time, he is the observer of that unique vision. He is required, finally, to be a creator, the architect of a new poetic universe, in which all components of his vision are united, in a harmonious entity.

We may describe this kind of structure as a theatrical realization of the "stream-of-consciousness." Miller's "stream-of-consciousness" differs in certain particulars from that of other dramatists such as Williams and O'Neill; it is, in many ways, close to that of novelists such as Virginia Woolf. For, like Woolf, Miller does not divide his vision of reality into discrete units—pictures with rigid boundaries. He, rather, conceives Willy's mind as a place "out of time," as a state in which all boundaries have been erased, in which all things are coexistent. He writes [in his introduction to *Collected Plays*]: "Above all, in the structural sense, I aimed to make a play with the veritable countenance of life. To make the one the many."

Now, the need to give such an ambiguous poetic perception a concrete form in the theatre has, obviously, presented the playwright with certain difficulties which other American dramatists have shared: How can "consciousness" be connoted on the stage? As in traditional tragedy, Miller projects his vision of experience by employing the method of poetry. *Death of a Salesman,* like *Prometheus Bound, Oedipus, King Lear,* or for that matter, like *Ghosts, The Cherry Orchard, The Ghost Sonata, The Hairy Ape, Our Town,* or *A Streetcar Named Desire,* is, thus, a kind of poem; that is to say, it represents the exposition of a key image, through the simultaneous realization of component figures. We have noted Miller's own comment on the central image of Willy's head, which opens up to reveal his "way of mind." He describes the play [in his introduction to *Collected Plays*] as a veritable "sea of images": shapes in the protagonist's vision:

> The play's eye was to revolve from within Willy's head, sweeping endlessly in all directions like a light on the sea, and nothing that formed in the distant mist was to be left uninvestigated. It was thought of as having the density of the novel form in its inter-

change of viewpoints, so that while all roads led to Willy the other characters were to feel it was their play, a story about them and not him. . . . There are no flashbacks in this play but only a mobile concurrency of past and present, and this, again, because in his desperation to justify his life Willy Loman has destroyed the boundaries between now and then.

Death of a Salesman is an aesthetic progression: a reconstruction of the movement of consciousness: the perception of facts, events, and ideas; fears, passions, and superstitions; hopes, dreams, and ambitions, in their various stages of maturity and immaturity. Clearly, this definition might easily apply to other contemporary arts, particularly, to the novel, the long poem, the modern dance, or the cinema. The significant factor which distinguishes *Death of a Salesman* from these related forms is the fact that it was written to be spoken and performed by live actors before a live audience. Miller speaks of drama as a symbolic ritual, which projects the spectator's consciousness into the mind of the protagonist, and which, in turn, introjects the suffering, enlightenment, and triumph of the protagonist into the consciousness of the spectator. Miller, like other contemporary dramatists, regards *spectacle* as a critical element of theatrical language. For it provides the poetic vision with its sensuous fabric, with its texture.

Miller, like other playwrights who have followed the theories and practice of Wagner, has given considerable attention to the articulation of an appropriate dramaturgy for the interpretation of his tragic myth. Much of the text of *Death of a Salesman* is given to the articulation of the sensuous form of the poetic image. The playwright's description of the setting follows:

> A melody is heard, played upon a flute. It is small and fine, telling of grass and trees and the horizon. The curtain rises.
>
> Before us is the Salesman's house. We are aware of towering, angular shapes behind it, surrounding it on all sides. Only the blue light of the sky falls upon the house and forestage; the surrounding area shows an angry glow of orange. As more light appears, we see a solid vault of apartment houses around the small, fragile-seeming home. An air of the dream clings to the place, a dream rising out of reality. . . .
>
> The entire setting is wholly or, in some places, partially transparent. The roof-line of the house is one-dimensional; under and over it we see the apartment buildings. Before the house lies an apron, curving beyond the forestage into the orchestra. This

forward area serves as the back yard as well as the locale of all
Willy's imaginings and of his city scenes. Whenever the action is
in the present the actors observe the imaginary wall-lines, enter-
ing the house only through its door at the left. But in the scenes
of the past these boundaries are broken, and characters enter or
leave a room by stepping "through" a wall onto the forestage.

Death of a Salesman is, then, an example of that kind of form which
Professor Francis Fergusson has described as "poetry in the theatre." It is a
myth which projects before the spectator an image of the protagonist's
consciousness. The playwright attempts to reveal a tragic progression within
the consciousness of the protagonist. He employs, as the instrumentation of
vision, a complex theatre symbol: a union of gesture, word, and music;
light, color, and pattern; rhythm and movement. We may now ask: What is
the nature of this myth? In what sense is it tragic?

III

Miller follows O'Neill in suggesting that suffering in the modern world
is often deceptively masked, inasmuch as it has been clearly removed from
the context of the purely physical. The contemporary protagonist Loman
suffers from such an ambiguous evil, from a malady which modern arts and
letters have determined the moral sickness of the twentieth century. Miller
describes this sickness as the "disease of unrelatedness." Its symptoms are a
sense of alienation, a loss of meaning, and a growing despair. We have seen
this illness personified in the protagonist throughout the contemporary
drama: in O'Neill's Yank, Williams's Blanche, in Wilder's Cain in *The Skin
of Our Teeth,* as well as in the protagonists of Odets, Saroyan, Hellman,
Hansberry, and, more recently, Albee and others. While other dramatists
are often equivocal in their assessment of causes, Miller is quite clear about
the roots of this sickness. He traces modern suffering to the ancient cause:
ignorance. *Death of a Salesman* attempts to trace Loman's progress from
ignorance, through the cycle of suffering, to enlightenment. As in Classic
tragedy, the price of this "Odyssey" is death, but, through his personal
sacrifice, the protagonist redeems his house and promises to his posterity yet
another chance.

Miller's transposition of the tragic movement to a "modern key" seems
effective. If there is a problem with his myth, it would seem to emanate from
his choice of Loman as protagonist; that is to say, with the idea of a truly
common man as tragic hero. For at first glance, Willy Loman, as a symbol
of modern man, seems to have critical shortcomings. To begin with, he does

not seem to have sinned greatly enough to satisfy the needs of tragic shock and terror. In this respect, Tennessee Williams's protagonists, with their sexual crimes, more nearly approach the Greek interpretation of man sickened by the horror of transgression. Miller's *hamartia* is more subtle than that of Williams, but perhaps even more Classic in its ultimate implications. For Miller, like Sophocles, insists that *tragic catastrophe* is the result of ignorance rather than the end of willful transgression. Loman's crime in the universe may be likened to that of Agamemnon or Lear; it is the appearance of indifference, the absence of sympathy, and the lack of a sense of moral law. For Miller, moral ignorance is, at once, the most serious—and most common—indictment against humanity in our time.

But there is, yet, a second and even more serious objection which may be raised against Loman as hero; and that is that he does not seem to measure up to the stature of a great and good man. Against the outline of Oedipus, Lear, or Faust, Loman appears a small man, a mere failure, who does not have sufficient grace to warrant universal concern. Again, appearances belie the truth. For Loman, Miller holds, is the measure of certain changes in value associated with the rise of a democratic society. It is, according to the playwright, Loman who is the symbol of the most powerful moral force in the modern world: the common man. It is, the playwright continues, the outcome of the crisis within his consciousness which will, with certainty, determine the disposition of the moral dilemma which still grips the human race. But Miller, the American, goes even further in the justification of his protagonist. For, he declares, not only must a contemporary tragic myth mirror the shape of transgression and the nature of power in our age, it ought, also, to be the measure of our ethical advance over prior civilizations. If the Greek hero mirrored a society which condoned slavery, and the Renaissance protagonist represented an aristocratic minority, Willy Loman is the measure of democracy's promise of unlimited human possibility. He is the representative of an open order where all values—even virtue—may be gained at any moment when man is willing to risk commitment.

It is clear that, for Miller, Loman is a virtuous man; that is to say, he wins virtue, in a moment released from the boundaries of time and causality. Miller, like the existentialists, defines virtue, heroism, and nobility, in anti-Aristotelian terms; that is to say, Loman's character is not a static arrangement of fixed virtues. On the contrary, the protagonist gains ultimate value in the universe at the same instant when he commits himself to the search for truth, in that "existential moment" which the play itself represents. Loman, the contemporary hero, embarks upon a most courageous "Odyssey": the descent into the self, where he engages his most dangerous enemy, himself. The fact that he does so late in his life does not, in the contemporary context, diminish his value. For Loman, like Lear, is a hero who comes late in the tragic progression to enlightenment.

Miller attempts to take his tragic cycle to its natural conclusion by giving a sign to the protagonist's victory. In *Death of a Salesman,* as in traditional tragedy, the sign is itself a paradox. Loman's suicide, like Oedipus's self-blinding or Antigone's self-murder, is obviously intended as a gesture of the hero's victory over circumstances. It is an act of love, intended to redeem his house. Willy's wife indicates this interpretation in the Requiem:

> Forgive me, dear, I can't cry. I don't know what it is, but I can't cry. I don't understand it. Why did you ever do that? Help me, Willy, I can't cry. It seems to me that you're just on another trip. I keep expecting you. Willy, dear, I can't cry. Why did you do it? I search and search and I search, and I can't understand it, Willy. I made the last payment on the house today. Today, dear. And there'll be nobody home . . . We're free and clear . . . We're free . . . We're free . . . We're free . . .

Arthur Miller's *Death of a Salesman* is, perhaps, to this time, the most mature example of a myth of contemporary life. The chief value of this drama is its attempt to reveal those ultimate meanings which are resident in modern experience. Perhaps the most significant comment on this play is not its literary achievement, as such, but is, rather, the impact which it has had on spectators, both in America and abroad. The influence of this drama, first performed in 1949, continues to grow in world theatre. For it articulates, in language which can be appreciated by popular audiences, certain new dimensions of the human dilemma. The playwright's own words [in his introduction to *Collected Plays*] would seem to summarize the achievement of this myth about modern life:

> The ultimate justification for a genuine new form is the new and heightened consciousness it creates and makes possible—a consciousness of causation in the light of known but hitherto inexplicable effects.

CLINTON W. TROWBRIDGE

Arthur Miller: Between Pathos and Tragedy

No one in the American theater today speaks as passionately and as idealistically about the possibilities of drama as Arthur Miller:

> There lies within the dramatic form the ultimate possibility of raising the truth-consciousness of mankind to a level of such intensity as to transform those who observe it,

wrote Miller in 1956. While he was still an undergraduate at the University of Michigan in the 1930s, he dedicated himself to the task of creating such a drama:

> With the greatest of presumption, (he wrote about his earliest ambitions), I conceived that the great writer was the destroyer of chaos, a man privy to the council of the hidden gods who administer the hidden laws that bind us all and destroy us all if we do not know them.

What might be called Miller's commitment to greatness is important to recognize at the outset because it is this that has made him so harshly critical of the modern theater, has driven him to use his talents only for the production of what he considers the highest in dramatic art, and it is this, finally, that has brought him the extraordinary mixture of critical praise and scorn that he has received.

Miller's primary criticism of the American theater is that it has sepa-

From *Modern Drama* 10, no. 3 (December 1967). © 1967 by the University of Toronto, Graduate Centre for the Study of Drama.

39

rated the individual from his society and in doing so has merely dramatized
man's alienation from the world in which he lives:

> Since 1920, (he wrote in 1953), American drama has been a
> steady year by year documentation of the frustration of man. I
> do not believe in this. . . . That is not our fate.

More recently Miller added:

> The fifties became an era of gauze. Tennessee Williams is respon-
> sible for this in the main. One of my own feet stands in this
> stream. It is a cruel, romantic neuroticism, a translation of cur-
> rent life into the war within the self. All conflict tends to be
> transformed into sexual conflict. . . . It is a theatre with the
> blues. . . . The drama will have to re-address itself to the world
> beyond the senses, to fate.

In spite of what he says about his own participation in such a theater,
Miller has from the beginning addressed himself to the world beyond the
senses. All of his plays depict characters who struggle against fate, though
in the earlier plays "fate" means the economic, political, and social forces of
their times.

Because of Miller's acknowledgement of Ibsen as his earliest master (he
wrote an adaptation of *An Enemy of the People* in 1951), and because his
original concern was to depict man in conflict with his society, it is not
surprising that he has been most often thought of as a writer of problem
plays, a latter day Ibsen, whose messages cease to excite with the passing of
the problem with which they deal. But such a judgment is as unfair to Miller
as it is to Ibsen; and to Miller, at least, it reflects the anti-intellectual bias of
the times. Of this bias Miller has spoken continually and vehemently. An-
swering a criticism of Peter Ustinov, Miller wrote in 1960:

> I am not calling for more ideology, as Ustinov implies. I am
> simply asking for a theatre in which an adult who wants to live
> can find plays that will heighten his awareness of what living in
> our time involves. I am tired of a theatre of sensation, that's all.
> I am tired of seeing man as merely a bundle of nerves. That way
> lies pathology, and we have pretty much arrived.

Having in mind his own attempts in *The Crucible,* Miller wrote of the
difficulties involved in depicting the thinking man on the stage:

> In our drama the man with convictions has in the past been a
> comic figure. I believe he fits in our drama more now, though,

and I am trying to find a way, a form, a method of depicting people who do think.

Since that time he has gone further, and in *After the Fall* the entire action of the play takes place "in the mind, thought and memory" of its intellectual protagonist. Judging from the critical reception given that work, it would seem that Miller's hope of thirteen years ago was all too optimistic and that people who do think are simply unfit theatrical subjects. But more of this later. It is time to proceed to the question with which this paper deals: has Miller succeeded in dramatizing "what living in our time involves," and has he done so with such power as "to transform the truth consciousness of mankind"?

This may seem an unfair question to ask of any writer, but Miller himself demands that he be judged in such terms: "I ask of a play," he writes, "first, the dramatic question. . . . Second, the human question— What is its ultimate relevancy to the survival of the race?" For Miller the only drama that can so powerfully engage us as to transform our characters is tragedy. Its archenemy is pathos. For this reason it is natural that we should consider Miller's plays in view of these two terms.

Miller first raised the question of the writing of modern tragedy in his preface to *Death of a Salesman* in 1949. Most of us are familiar with his argument for the non-aristocratic tragic hero, the protagonist as common man, raised above his fellows not by rank or position but by the nobility of his spirit. More important for our purposes is his distinction between pathos and tragedy in the same preface.

> The possibility of victory must be there in tragedy. Where pathos rules, where pathos is finally derived, a character has fought a battle he could not possibly have won. The pathetic is achieved when the protagonist is, by virtue of his witlessness, his insensitivity, or the very air he gives off, incapable of grappling with a much superior force. Pathos truly is the mode for the pessimist. But tragedy requires a nicer balance between what is possible and what is impossible. And it is curious, although edifying, that the plays we revere, century after century, are the tragedies. In them, and in them alone, lies the belief—optimistic, if you will, in the perfectability of man.

The explanation of this "optimism" lies in Miller's understanding of the so-called tragic flaw. Far from being a fault, it is envisioned as that very strength of will that makes the protagonist refuse "to remain passive in the face of what he conceives to be a challenge to his dignity, his image of his rightful status."

It is not Miller's theory of tragedy that I want to discuss here, however. Rather, I would draw attention to one characteristic of tragedy that for Miller, at least, is essential. It is the idea that tragedy deals ultimately with paradox. On the one hand, it posits the destruction of the hero; its line of action must be, in fact, one in which the sense of doom grows stronger and stronger. On the other hand, we must never for a moment regard the tragic hero's struggle against his fate as absurd, which would be the case if his destruction were completely inevitable. The essential paradox of tragedy, then, lies in the fact that even though the tragic hero is destroyed, his struggle "demonstrates the indestructible will of man to achieve his humanity."

> A great drama [Miller writes, almost mystically], is a great ju-
> risprudence. Balance is all. It will evade us until we can once
> again see man as whole, until sensitivity and power, justice and
> necessity are utterly face to face; until authority's justifications
> and rebellion's too are tracked even to those heights where the
> breath fails, where—because the largest point of view as well as
> the smaller has spoken—truly the rest is silence.

Pathos is "that counterfeit of meaning" because, in addition to stacking the cards against the protagonist, it does not push the dramatic question far enough; it settles for a vision of mankind that is oversimplified and for that reason can have no real power over us.

Nothing is clearer from a study of Miller's plays than the fact of his growth toward tragedy, as he conceives it, and away from pathos, and one way of seeing this growth is to compare the manner in which Miller has handled the problem of dramatic resolution. In *All My Sons,* the resolution of the basic dramatic conflict is clearly stated in the title. Joe Keller, who has thought that there was nothing bigger than the family, comes to the realization that the pilots who died as the result of the faulty engine heads shipped by his factory were "all my sons." As a direct and immediate result of this knowledge, he commits suicide. *All My Sons* never passes beyond its very considerable pathos to tragedy because, for one thing, it resolves its basic dramatic conflict too simply and in so doing falsifies the paradox that lies unexamined at its heart. How can a person keep his sense of right and wrong while grappling for a living in a business world which recognizes only the principle of the survival of the fittest? It was this question, basic to, though hardly even considered in, *All My Sons* that Miller made the central one in his next, and most widely acclaimed, play, *Death of a Salesman.*

Whereas in *All My Sons*, father and son stood in ideological opposition to each other and so represented the conflicting values that formed the dramatic question of the play, in *Death of a Salesman* the father and the older son, Biff, though antagonists, are more closely related in their values and there is thus more sense of paradox in the resolution of the basic dramatic conflict. Joe Keller lived by the wrong values, and though the question of what the right values are was only superficially examined, we could at least see that his suicide was a logical result of his self-knowledge. On the other hand, Biff Loman's statement about his father: "He had the wrong dreams. All, all wrong" has to be considered in the light of the neighbor Charlie's answer: "A salesman is got to dream, boy. It comes with the territory" and with the heart-rending urging of Willie's wife: "Attention must be paid. . . . There's more good in him than in many other people." Willie, though he has moments of partial awareness, never does learn that he has lived all, all wrong: and thus the dramatic question of the play remains unresolved. Yet his death is ironic as well as far more full of pathos than Joe's because in depicting it as the result of love as well as imagining it as the final act of a man who literally *is* worth more dead than alive, Miller has remained true to the paradox that lies at the basis of the play.

Powerful as *Death of a Salesman* is, however, Miller himself felt that the play did not succeed in passing beyond pathos into tragedy. A few years after the writing of *Death of a Salesman* he wrote:

> There is great danger in pathos, which can destroy any tragedy if you let it go far enough. My weakness is that I can create pathos at will. It is one of the easiest things to do. I feel that Willie Loman lacks sufficient insight into this situation which would have made him a greater, more significant figure.

We might add that Willie could be taken as almost the model for the protagonist who is "by virtue of his witlessness, his insensitivity, or the very air he gives off, incapable of grappling with a much superior force."

Death of a Salesman is one of the enduring plays of our time, but its strength lies more in its ability to stir our pity than our fear. With his next play Miller found a subject that came nearer his concept of tragedy. *The Crucible,* as Miller tells us,

> developed from a paradox . . . in whose grip we still live, and there is no prospect yet that we will discover its resolution. The witch hunt was a perverse manifestation of the panic which set in among all classes when the balance began to turn toward

greater individual freedom. When one rises above the individual villainy displayed, one can only pity them all, just as we shall be pitied someday. It is still impossible for man to organize his social life without repressions, and the balance has yet to be struck between order and freedom.

Written at the time of the McCarthy hearings, *The Crucible* calls up fear as well as pity, however. More aware of what they were doing than were any of Miller's earlier protagonists, the people of Salem are much closer to his concept of the tragic hero. Particularly is this so with John Proctor, the chief protagonist, whose final words are spoken out of the agonizing awareness of corporate guilt. To the court, that has condemned him as well as other innocent people, he cries:

> For them that quail to bring man out of ignorance, as I have quailed and as you quail now when you know in all your black hearts that this be fraud—God damns our kind especially, and we will burn, we will burn together.

In *The Crucible* there is also, for the first time in Miller's work, a genuine sense of exaltation; for in the struggles of John Proctor and the other martyrs to the cause of justice, we recognize our own victory over some of the worst elements of our Puritan past. *The Crucible* has, in fact, virtually all of the characteristics of successful tragedy as Miller conceives them to be. Yet it cannot be said to reach "those heights where the breath fails" because it lacks something far more important to drama: that sense of vividly and fully imagined character that made of Willie Loman a kind of modern Everyman. George Jean Nathan, while overstating the case against Miller, recognized this essential failure in the play when he wrote that the couple who fall victim to the persecution exist mainly as a vehicle for Miller's ideas and that "their tragedy accordingly has the distant air of a dramatic recitation rather than of any personal suffering."

We need not consider Miller's next work, *A Memory of Two Mondays,* a sentimentalized and nostalgic one-act play about a young working man who is saving up his money to go to college. *A View from the Bridge,* however, written at the same time, is of prime importance, for it shows a profound change in Miller's concept of fate.

In the earlier plays fate took the form of the social, economic, or political forces of society. In Eddie Carbone's tragic fall, however, Miller sees for the first time the presence of a quite different force; for Eddie's struggle is not primarily with his society but with himself, with a passion that he can neither understand nor control. Like Phaedra, Eddie is possessed by an unnatural and all devouring love, though unlike Phaedra he is never aware of the true nature of his feelings. In his preface to *A View from the Bridge,* Miller draws attention to the classical outlines of the story:

> When I heard the tale first it seemed to me that it must be some re-enactment of a Greek myth which was ringing a long buried bell in my own subconscious mind. . . . It is not designed primarily to draw tears or laughter from an audience but to strike a particular note of astonishment at the way in which, and the reasons for which, a man will endanger and risk and lose his very life.

Eddie Carbone, unable to give up his niece to one of his wife's illegally entered immigrant cousins whom they are sheltering from the authorities, informs on them and, in so doing, betrays the mores of the society in which he lives. Miller has centered his attention, however, not on Eddie's struggle against society but on his defiance of nature. The lawyer, Alfieri, whose manner of expression as well as admonitory function on the play suggests the *choragus* of Greek tragedy, warns Eddie not to interfere with Catherine and Rudolpho:

> The law is nature.
> The law is only a word for what has a right to happen.
> When the law is wrong it's because it's unnatural.
> But in this case it is natural
> And a river will drown you
> If you buck it now.
> Let her go. And bless her.

Eddie thinks he is only protecting his niece from an unworthy husband, but his classical prototype, the Oedipus whose name his own suggests, looms larger and larger until, at the end of the play, after Eddie has been killed in a knife fight with Rudolpho's brother, the lawyer, Alfieri, can draw a parallel between Eddie and the protagonists of Greek tragedy and comment on man's apparently unchangeable primitive nature.

This identifying of fate with the natural law represents an important turning point in Miller's concept of tragedy, but it is not until *After the Fall* that we see him making full use of this concept to create in us the exaltation of high tragedy. *A View from the Bridge,* powerful as it is, simply does not have the dimensions of tragedy. Its protagonist is even more unaware of what is happening to him than was Willie Loman, and therefore the physical

violence with which the play ends is more suggestive of the horrors of the
vendetta than of anything else. Astonishment is not, after all, the tragic
emotion, and although Miller has significantly broadened his concept of
fate, and in so doing has paved the way for the enlarged vision of *After the
Fall*, *A View from the Bridge* stands as the nearest thing to melodrama he
has yet written. The revisions Miller made in the play for its New York run
in 1965–1966, while they deepen its thematic content, cannot be said to
alter its basic dramatic vision.

We need not pause long over Miller's next work, *The Misfits*, though
it is certainly rich in dramatic content (Every character is eventually put into
dramatic opposition with virtually every other.), and though it deals with an
extraordinary number of basic questions (What is the nature of innocence?
Can it, and if it can, should it be protected? Is communication between man
and man, man and society, man and the universe, man and himself either
possible or desirable? Is life worth living or not, and before we answer that
what do we mean by life and what do we mean by living?), *The Misfits* need
not concern us here because of its hopefully-happy ending. Technically
speaking, it is neither pathos nor tragedy but comedy, and while Miller's
paean to marriage as the solution to all problems can be understood in the
light of the sun that was then illuminating his private life, as a dramatic
resolution the sentimental ending of *The Misfits* represents the triumph of
the soapbox over the stage.

It is all the more to Miller's credit that after mawkishly indulging his
romantic nature in *The Misfits*, he should have treated much the same
material with the dispassionate honesty that he displays in *After the Fall*.
Not that many critics saw it this way. Perhaps no recent play written by a
major playwright has received more critical abuse than *After the Fall*. "A
three-and-one-half hour breach of taste," wrote Robert Brustein of *The
New Republic*. Deploring its absence of meaning and lack of drama, Richard
Gilman of *Commonweal* found in it "only wind, shadows, and purple
smoke." The *New Yorker* did not deign to review it at all, but in a column
and a half of coldly factual prose attempted, apparently, to kill it by neglect.
Time magazine took the opposite approach and concluded its equally brief
review with these caustic words: "The code of the *Fall* is: when life seems
unbearable, find a new woman and start a new life." So hostile were most
of the reviews that Miller felt forced to answer his critics, and only ten days
after the play's opening published a moving and powerful defense of it in
Life magazine. In many ways it is fortunate that Miller was driven to such
a pass, for he not only showed how completely most of the reviewers had

misunderstood his intentions but provided us with an invaluable critical introduction to his work.

One thing Miller made most clear: he is more than ever the moralist. The moralist, moreover, who can afford to speak with the tone of the prophet, being convinced that he has discovered the hidden laws of the universe. "I believe *After the Fall*," he writes, "to be a dramatic statement of a hidden process which underlies the destructiveness hanging over this age." Man's complicity with evil, in himself and in his world, the fact of man's basically destructive nature and the sense of guilt that must follow that knowledge, this is the thematic content of Miller's play. None of us is innocent; we are all born after the fall. Only after facing the knowledge of our own defeat can we hope to progress; only after admitting our own evil can we work for our own good. It is this paradoxical vision that forms the heart of the play; and it is because Miller has forced this vision on us so relentlessly, with such dramatic intensity, that *After the Fall* can be said to be not only his greatest triumph but one of the few genuinely tragic plays of our time.

All of Miller's plays have been concerned with depicting man's relationship to the world he lives in. All of them have aimed at bringing mankind to a tragic vision of that relationship. Yet powerful as they all are in varying degrees, none of them successfully passed beyond pathos into tragedy. One reason for this is that not until *After the Fall* did Miller find a subject and a theme of genuinely tragic proportions.

Quentin is more than just the most intellectual of Miller's protagonists. He is a portrait of thinking man in our society, his tragic flaw (that which elevates him from his fellows) being his inability to lie to himself. "What's moral?" asks Maggie of him at one point in the play, and he replies: "To tell the truth, even against yourself." The truth that he discovers in himself and in his world is that all men are touched with guilt, that consequently it is impossible to see human life in terms of the war between the Good and the Evil. Even the Nazis, especially, the play seems to say, the Nazis, must be recognized as our brothers; for we are all capable of their atrocities. If no man can be wholly hated, it is equally true that no man can be wholly loved; and Quentin's desire to dispel the adoration of others is as strong as his search for the nature of his own guilt.

Powerful as the thematic content of the play is, however, what gives *After the Fall* its extraordinary intensity and its real dramatic significance is its form. The entire action of the play, as Miller tells us is in "the mind, thought and memory" of its protagonist, Quentin. Since Quentin is imagined as speaking to a silent figure in the audience whom Miller calls the

"Listener," there is a framing action to the play which is, in form, a monologue. Yet we could also call the frame of the play the soliloque, since, as Miller tells us, "The 'Listener,' who to some will be a psychoanalyst, to others God, is Quentin himself turned at the edge of the abyss to look at his own experience." Since the "Listener" is also, in many ways, identified with the audience, another way of conceiving of the frame is as a long aside. Not only is the very frame of the play a dramatic innovation which stirs our imagination and almost forces our involvement, but it provides what would seem to be the ultimate observation of the classical unities: a person's words, thoughts, and memories over a two-hour period during which he is imagined in conference with a silent figure.

Oppressed by the chaos in himself and in his time, Quentin has come to the "Listener" for advice. Having lived through two marriages and feeling as he does generally disillusioned about life, he is afraid to risk a third marriage. The agony he feels stems from his own sense of complicity with evil and his consequent inability to resolve the question of what his future should be. But his choice is not simply whether to marry or not to marry. Basically it is whether to be or not to be. Only at the end of the play does he make a choice. Another characteristic of the frame, then, is that it deals solely with the dramatic resolution of the play.

The real action of the play, of course, is not this framing action but is composed of the dramatized memories and thoughts that come to Quentin during his consultation with the "Listener." Here Miller seems to have realized the great possibilities of the flash-back technique that he so successfully employed in *Death of a Salesman*. The play takes almost twice as long to perform as his imagined conversation lasts, for as Quentin thinks or remembers, the scene from his past is reenacted on the stage. In fact, the significant moments from Quentin's life are presented before us, not in chronological order but in the more intense psychological order of the association of ideas. He hears his brother's voice promising family support in the midst of a painful scene in which support is being withdrawn from him by someone else. His first wife appears on stage momentarily when his second wife unknowingly repeats her accusation. In some of these scenes from his past Quentin becomes so emotionally involved that we forget for the moment the frame of the play. In others he is the detached observer of a painful scene from his childhood, for instance; and this pulling of Quentin in and out of his own past, as it were, is itself intensely dramatic. Time, space, and action are as freely used in the play itself as they are compressed in the framing action, the very counterpoint between the apparent disorder and complexity of the one and the order and simplicity of the other adding still more to the dramatic intensity of the play. The great dramatic innovation of *After the Fall* consists of Miller's method here of juxtaposing scenes from Quentin's past one on the other so that finally his life has been revealed to us with all the richness that we usually associate with the novel as a form. The modern novelist, Joyce and Proust in particular, as well as creators of the modern film, seem to have given Miller what he has been looking for since 1963: "a form, a method of depicting people who do think."

At the end of the play Quentin knows little more about himself than he did at the beginning. After talking to the "Listener" for two hours, he simply feels less afraid of life and has very hesitantly decided to risk another marriage. Our knowledge of him, however, and of life through him, is so deep as to approach wonder. Identified dramatically as we are in part with the "Listener," we partake of his seeming omniscience. Miller once wrote that the central question asked by all serious drama is "How may a man make of the outside world a home?" Miller treats us and our world with such determined honesty and such intellectual scope that *After the Fall* can be said to give an answer to that question, an answer that Quentin characteristically puts in the form of a series of questions to the "Listener" at the end of the play:

> I swear to you, I could love this world again! . . . Is the knowing all? To know, and even happily, that we meet unblessed; not in some garden of wax fruit and painted trees, that lie of Eden, but after the Fall, after many, many deaths. Is the knowing all? . . . And the wish to kill is never killed, but with some gift of courage one may look into its face when it appears, and with a stroke of love—as to an idiot in the house—forgive it; again and again . . . forever? . . . No, it's not certainty, I don't feel that. But it does seem feasible . . . not to be afraid. Perhaps it's all one has.

Essential as the form of *After the Fall* is to the realization of its power as drama, it would have little effect if Miller had not been able to create convincing characters as well. Perhaps the greatest tribute to Miller's powers of characterization in this play is the very fact that he succeeded in shocking so many in his use of his former wife Marilyn Monroe as the basis for the character of Maggie. No one is shocked by a weak characterization, no matter how recognizable the original. Were she more aware of what was happening to her, she might have taken on the proportions of a tragic heroine. As it is she stands above Willie Loman even as Miller's most fully realized and completely human figure of pathos.

"A great drama is a great jurisprudence. Balance is all," Miller wrote.

In no other play of recent times has such a balance been struck as in *After the Fall,* a balance between the forces of hate and the forces of love, between despair and hope, a balance, finally, between pity and fear, the union of which produces the exaltation of great tragedy, tragedy that has the power to carry us both nearer to and beyond ourselves, tragedy that because it envisions man in ultimate conflict with the demon in himself can hope to rid him of that demon, can hope to raise "the truth-consciousness of mankind to a level of such intensity as to transform those who observe it." Miller himself has called *After the Fall* his "happiest" work. Elia Kazan saw it as "one of the few truly great plays with which he has come in contact." Howard Taubman of the *New York Times* found the play to be "Miller's maturest."

Coming, as it does, less than a year after *After the Fall,* Miller's most recent play, *Incident at Vichy,* seems particularly disappointing. Generally recognized as the most obtrusively didactic of all of his plays, it is neither pathos nor tragedy but, rather, a dramatized essay on the same subject of universal human guilt that had been so powerfully treated in the earlier play. The characters are little more than spokesmen for different points of view, and though intellectual stimulation and a degree of dramatic intensity results from the clash of ideas, the play as such is certainly Miller's least dramatic.

It remains to be seen whether Miller's next play will reach the tragic heights of *After the Fall.* As his career now stands, he hovers between pathos and tragedy, our most important and our most serious playwright.

ORM ÖVERLAND

The Action and Its Significance:
Arthur Miller's Struggle with Dramatic Form

"There are two questions I ask myself over and over when I'm work-ing," Arthur Miller has remarked. "What do I mean? What am I trying to say?" The questions do not cease when a play is completed but continue to trouble him. In the introduction to his *Collected Plays* Miller is constantly asking of each play: "What did I mean? What was I trying to say?" These questions and the playwright's attempts to answer them are directly related to his account of how he planned and wrote his next play.

The process of playwriting is given a peculiar wavelike rhythm in Mil-ler's own story of his efforts to realize his intentions from one play to the other. Troughs of dejection on being exposed to unexpected critical and audience responses to a newly completed play are followed by swells of creativity informed by the dramatist's determination to make himself more clearly understood in the next one. This wavelike rhythm of challenge and response is the underlying structural principle of Miller's introduction to his *Collected Plays*. Behind it one may suspect the workings of a radical distrust of his chosen medium. The present essay will consider some of the effects both of this distrust of the theater as a means of communication and of Miller's theories of dramatic form on his career as a dramatist.

Arthur Miller is not alone in asking what he is trying to say in his plays, nor in being concerned that they may evoke other responses than those the playwright thought he had aimed at. From the early reviews of *Death of a Salesman* critics have observed that a central problem in the

From *Modern Drama* 18, no. 1 (March 1975). © 1975 by the University of Toronto, Graduate Centre for the Study of Drama.

evaluation of Miller's work is a conflict of themes, real or apparent, within each play.

The case for the prosecution has been well put by Eric Bentley:

> Mr. Miller says he is attempting a synthesis of the social and the psychological, and, though one may not see any synthesis, one certainly sees the thesis and the antithesis. In fact, one never knows what a Miller play is about: politics or sex. If *Death of a Salesman* is political, the key scene is the one with the tape recorder; if it's sexual, the key scene is the one in the Boston hotel. You may say of *The Crucible* that it isn't about McCarthy, it's about love in the seventeenth century. And you may say of *A View from the Bridge* that it isn't about informing, it's about incest and homosexuality.

John Mander points to the same conflict in his analysis of *Death of a Salesman* in his *The Writer and Commitment:*

> If we take the "psychological" motivation as primary, the "social" documentation seems gratuitous, if we take the "social" documentation as primary, the "psychological" motivation seems gratuitous. And we have, I am convinced, to choose which kind of motivation must have the priority; we cannot have both at once.

Mr. Mander's own image of this conflict of themes within Arthur Miller's play is the house divided and its two incompatible masters are Freud and Marx.

More sympathetic critics find that the plays successfully embody the author's intentions of dramatizing a synthesis of the two kinds of motivation. Edward Murray, for instance, has made the same observation as have Bentley and Mander, but in his view the difficulty of branding Miller either a "social" or a "psychological" dramatist points to a strength rather than to a flaw in his work: "At his best, Miller has avoided the extremes of clinical psychiatric case studies on the one hand and mere sociological reports on the other. . . . he has indicated . . . how the dramatist might maintain in delicate balance both personal and social motivation."

Miller himself has often spoken of modern drama in general and his own in particular in terms of a split between the private and the social. In the 1956 essay "The Family in Modern Drama," he claims that the various forms of modern drama "express human relationships of a particular kind, each of them suited to express either a primarily familial relation at one extreme, or a primarily social relation at the other." At times he has pointed to his own affinity with one or the other of these two extreme points of view on human relationships, as when he talks of the forties and fifties as "an era of gauze," for which he finds Tennessee Williams mainly responsible: "One of my own feet stands in this stream. It is a cruel, romantic neuroticism, a translation of current life into the war within the self. The personal has triumphed. All conflict tends to be transformed into sexual conflict." More often, as in "The Shadow of the Gods," Miller has seen himself primarily in the social tradition of the thirties. It is in this essay that Miller makes one of his most explicit statements on the need for a synthesis of the two approaches:

> Society is inside of man and man is inside society, and you cannot even create a truthfully drawn psychological entity on the stage until you understand his social relations and their power to make him what he is and to prevent him from being what he is not. The fish is in the water and the water is in the fish.

Such synthesis, however, is fraught with problems which are closely connected with Miller's medium, the theater.

Indeed, for Miller synthesis has largely been a question of dramatic form, and the problem for the playwright has been to create a viable form that could bridge "the deep split between the private life of man and his social life." In addition to his frustration with audience responses and his desire to make himself more clearly understood, part of the momentum behind Miller's search for new and more satisfactory modes of expression after the realistic *All My Sons* has been the conviction that the realistic mode in drama was an expression of "the family relationship within the play" while "the social relationship within the play" evoked the un-realistic modes.

In retrospect Miller found that the theme of *All My Sons* (1947) "is the question of actions and consequences," and the play dramatizes this theme in the story of Joe Keller, for whom there was nothing bigger than the family, and his son Chris, for whom "one new thing was made" out of the destruction of the war: "A kind of—responsibility. Man for man." When Miller is slightly dissatisfied with his first successful play, it is because he believes that he had allowed the impact of what he calls one kind of "morality" to "obscure" the other kind "in which the play is primarily interested." These two kinds of "morality" are closely related to the two kinds of "motivation"—psychological and social—that John Mander and other critics have pointed to. The problem may be seen more clearly by observing that the play has two centers of interest. The one, in which Miller claims "the play is primarily interested," is intellectual, the other emotional. The former is mainly expressed through the play's dialogue, the latter is more deeply embedded in the action itself.

Joe Keller gradually emerges as a criminal. He has sold defective cylinder heads to the air force during the war and was thus directly responsible for the deaths of twenty-one pilots. The horror of this deed is further brought home to the audience by the discovery that Keller's elder son was a pilot lost in action. This is what we may call the emotional center of interest, and most of the plot is concerned with this past crime and its consequences for Keller and his family. But it is this emotional center that for Miller obscures the real meaning of the play.

Miller wanted his play to be about "unrelatedness":

> Joe Keller's trouble, in a word, is not that he cannot tell right from wrong but that his cast of mind cannot admit that he, personally, has any viable connection with his world, his universe, or his society. . . . In this sense Joe Keller is a threat to society and in this sense the play is a social play. Its "socialness" does not reside in its having dealt with the crime of selling defective materials to a nation at war—the same crime could easily be the basis of a thriller which would have no place in social dramaturgy. It is that the crime is seen as having roots in a certain relationship of the individual to society, and to a certain indoctrination he embodies, which, if dominant, can mean a jungle existence for all of us no matter how high our buildings soar.

This, then, is the intellectual center of the play. Any good drama needs to engage the intellect as well as the emotions of its audience. Miller's problem is that these two spheres in *All My Sons* are not concentric. When a play has two centers of interest at odds with each other, the emotional one will often, as here, have a more immediate impact on the audience because it is more intimately related to the action of the play. Invariably action takes precedence over the sophistication of dialogue or symbols.

Death of a Salesman (1949) may serve as further illustration of the point made about the two centers of interest in *All My Sons*. Bentley wrote that the key scene of the play could be the one in Howard Wagner's office or the one in the hotel room depending on whether the play was "political" or "sexual." There is no doubt, however, as to which scene has the greater impact in the theater. The hotel room scene is carefully prepared for. The

constant references to stockings and the growing tension around the repeated queries about what had happened to Biff after he had gone to ask his
father's advice in Boston are some of the factors that serve to highlight this
scene. A more immediate impression is made on the audience by the mys-
terious laughter and the glimpse of a strange woman quite early in the first
act. The point is, however, that it is primarily on the stage that this scene
makes such an overwhelming impact that it tends to overshadow the other
scenes that together make up the total image of Willy's plight. If the play is
read, if one treats it as one would a novel, balance is restored and a good
case may be made for a successful synthesis of "psychological" and "social"
motivation as argued, for instance, by Edward Murray.

Miller seems to have become increasingly aware of the difficulty of
making a harmonious whole of his vehicle and his theme. His story would
have sexual infidelity (consider for instance the prominence this factor must
have in any brief retelling of the plot of *Death of a Salesman* or *The Crucible*) or another personal moral failure at its center, while the significance
the story held for the author had to do with man's relationship to society,
to the outside world. The one kind of "morality" continues to obscure the
other. When starting out to write *A View from the Bridge* (1955), Miller
had almost despaired of making himself understood in the theater: no "reviews, favorable or not," had mentioned what he had considered the main
theme of *The Crucible* (1953). Since he, apparently, could not successfully
merge his plots and his intended themes, he arrived at a scheme that on the
face of it seems preposterous: he would "separate, openly and without
concealment, the action of the next play, *A View from the Bridge,* from its
generalized significance."

With such an attitude to the relationship between story and theme or
"action" and "significance" there is little wonder that Miller was prone to
writing plays where critics felt there was a conflict of themes. For while
Miller's imagination generates plots along psychoanalytic lines, his intellect
leans towards socioeconomic explanations.

The story was, according to his own account, his starting point for *A
View from the Bridge*:

> I had heard its story years before, quite as it appears in the play,
> and quite as complete. . . . It was written experimentally not
> only as a form, but as an exercise in interpretation. I found in
> myself a passionate detachment toward its story as one does
> toward a spectacle in which one is not engaged but which holds
> a fascination deriving from its monolithic perfection. If this had

> happened, and if I could not forget it after so many years, *there must be some meaning in it for me, and I could write what had happened, why it had happened, and to one side, as it were, express as much as I knew of my sense of its meaning for me. Yet I wished to leave the action intact so that the onlooker could seize the right to interpret it entirely for himself and to accept or reject my reading of its significance.* [my italics]

This decision, Miller explains, led to the creation of "the engaged narrator," the role played by Alfieri in *A View from the Bridge*.

The narrator is hardly an innovation in the history of dramatic literature, especially when seen in relation to the chorus in Greek drama. In our own time widely different playwrights like Thornton Wilder (*Our Town*) and Bertolt Brecht (*The Caucasian Chalk Circle*) have made successful use of the narrator. Such historical antecedents and the widespread use of narrators in modern drama should not be lost sight of when considering this aspect of Arthur Miller's plays. Miller's narrators, however, are closely connected with his reluctance to let his plays speak for themselves. They are born from his long and troubled struggle with dramatic form.

Arthur Miller had tried his hand at fiction as well as drama before he achieved success on Broadway with *All My Sons* in 1947. When he thought of his next play, his aim was to achieve "the density of the novel form in its interchange of viewpoints." Again and again he comments on *Death of a Salesman* in terms of a prose narrative, as when he contrasts its sense of time with that of *All My Sons:* "This time, if I could, I would have *told the whole story* and set forth all the characters in one unbroken speech or even one sentence or a single flash of light. As I look at the play now its form seems the form of a confession, for that is *how it is told.*" [my italics] Although this may merely be a manner of speaking, as suggested by his own critique of the movie version where "drama becomes narrative," it does point to an attitude that in certain respects runs counter to drama: the story as something to be *told* as opposed to something to be *shown* or dramatised.

In fact, however, *Death of a Salesman* succeeds precisely because Willy's story is shown on the stage, not told. The possible uncertainty as to motivation does not detract from the intense and unified impact of the drama in the theater. The characters reveal themselves through action and dialogue supported by what Miller has called the play's "structural images." All the more striking then, the need Miller evidently felt to have the characters stand forth and give their various interpretations of Willy's life after the drama proper has closed with Willy's death. The choruslike effect of the

"Requiem" is obviously related to Miller's conscious effort to write a tragedy of "the common man," a drama which places man in his full social context, which in his essay "On Social Plays" is so clearly associated in Miller's mind with Greek drama. From another point of view the "Requiem" may also be seen as the embryo of the narrator figure who becomes so conspicuous in *A View from the Bridge* and *After the Fall:* after the play is over the characters stand forth and tell the audience what the play is about.

Miller's reluctance to let a play speak for itself became even more evident in his two attempts to add extra material to the original text of *The Crucible* after its first production in 1953. The first of these additions, a second scene in act 2, helps to explain Abigail's behavior in act 3, but, as Laurence Olivier told the playwright, it is not necessary. Although Abigail's psychotic character is brought out entirely in action and dialogue, in an encounter with John Proctor on the eve of the trial, and there is no suggestion of extra-dramatic exposition, the added scene is nevertheless evidence of Miller's sense of not having succeeded in making himself understood in the original version of the play.

More striking is the evidence provided by the series of non-dramatic interpolated passages in the first act, where the playwright takes on the roles of historian, novelist and literary critic, often all at once, speaking himself *ex cathedra* rather than through his characters *ex scena*. There is an obvious difference in intent as well as effect in writing an introductory essay to one's play and writing a series of comments that are incorporated in the text itself. The material used need not be different. For example, some of the comments on Danforth in the introduction to the *Collected Plays* are quite similar to those on Parris or Hale incorporated in the play. In the one instance, however, he is looking at his play from the outside, as one of its many critics, in the other he has added new material to the play and has thus changed the text.

In effect the play has a narrator, not realized as a character but present as a voice commenting on the characters and the action and making clear some of the moral implications for the reader/audience. The director of the 1958 off-Broadway revival for *The Crucible* drew the consequences of the revised text and introduced "a narrator, called The Reader, to set the scenes and give the historical background of the play." Besides his function as one of the minor characters, this is what Alfieri does in *A View from the Bridge*. The introduction of a "narrator" element in *The Crucible* is closely related to Miller's attempts to have a separate voice present the author's view of the "generalized significance" of the "action" in the later play.

The interpolated expository passages of *The Crucible* serve two different purposes. Frequently the comments on a character merely repeat points
made in that part of the drama which may be acted on the stage. Indeed, the
opening words of the following paragraph on John Proctor are suggestive of
the Victorian novelist guiding his readers through his story, making sure
that no point, however obvious, may be missed:

> But as we shall see, the steady manner he displays does not
> spring from an untroubled soul. He is a sinner, a sinner not only
> against the moral fashion of the time, but against his own vision
> of decent conduct. These people had no ritual for the washing
> away of sins. It is another trait we inherited from them, and it
> has helped to discipline us as well as to breed hypocrisy among
> us. Proctor, respected and even feared in Salem, has come to
> regard himself as a kind of fraud. But no hint of this has yet
> appeared on the surface, and as he enters from the crowded
> parlor below it is a man in his prime we see, with a quiet con-
> fidence and an unexpressed, hidden force. Mary Warren, his
> servant, can barely speak for embarrassment and fear.

Proctor's sense of guilt is central to any understanding of him as a dramatic
character, but certainly this is made sufficiently clear by, for instance, the
several explicit remarks made by Elizabeth as well as by his behavior on the
stage.

While such passages are further instances of Miller's apparent distrust
of his medium as a means of communication, other passages speak of an
impatience with the limitations of the dramatic form. Miller had researched
this play thoroughly, and it is as if on second thought he has regretted that
he had not been able to bring as much of his research and his historical
insights into the play as he would have liked. But when he in the interpolated passages takes on the roles of historian and biographer he tends to
confuse the sharp line that must be drawn between the characters in a play
called *The Crucible* and a group of late seventeenth century individuals
bearing the same names as these characters. Thus, in the first of the two
paragraphs that serve to introduce Proctor as he enters on the stage, Miller
tells us:

> Proctor was a farmer in his middle thirties. He need not have
> been a partisan of any faction in the town, but there is evidence
> to suggest that he had a sharp and biting way with hypocrites.
> He was the kind of man—powerful of body, even-tempered, and

not easily led—who cannot refuse support to partisans without drawing their deepest resentment. In Proctor's presence a fool felt his foolishness instantly—and a Proctor is always marked for calumny therefore.

The change in tense in the paragraph that follows (quoted above) suggests that Miller had a different Proctor in mind in each paragraph: the historical Proctor and the character in the play. This confusion runs through the various character sketches or brief essays on for instance Parris, Putnam and Rebecca and Francis Nurse. It should further be noted that these interpolated expository passages are often concerned with motivation, and that both psychological, religious and socioeconomic explanations of the trials are given. While the information is interesting in itself and throws light on the Salem trials, it cannot add to our understanding of the drama as acted on the stage. Whatever needs to be known about these characters and their motives by the audience must be expressed in action and dialogue. That is, if we do not accept the dichotomy of "action" and "significance," with the latter element presented by a representative of the author, a "Reader" or a narrator.

The assumption of such a dichotomy, according to Miller, lies at the heart of the structure of his next play, *A View from the Bridge.* Here, and in *A Memory of Two Mondays,* the one-act play originally presented on the same play bill, Miller thinks of himself as having followed "the impulse to present rather than to represent an interpretation of reality. Incident and character are set forth with the barest naïveté, and action is stopped abruptly while commentary takes its place." On the face of it, however, it is difficult to see why such commentary should be found necessary, unless the playwright had given up trying to make himself understood through "action" alone or, rather, to let his "action" carry the full weight of the "significance" he saw in it.

In his introduction [to the *Collected Plays*] Miller claims at the outset that his "approach to playwriting and the drama itself is organic," and he insists that "the play must be dramatic rather than narrative in concept and execution." When towards the end of the introduction he explains that "the organic impulse behind" his early plays was "split apart" in *A View from the Bridge,* it is as if he admits the failure of this approach. The organic structure of the early *All My Sons,* however, has already been questioned by Miller in his critique of its two centers of interest. As in this earlier play, the emotional center of *A View from the Bridge* is embedded in the action. But in the latter play Miller explains that he deliberately tried not to have the dialogue of the characters involved in the action carry any burden that goes beyond this action. The aspect of the play that dialogue attempted to express in *All My Sons* is now delegated to the narrator. The more explicit splitting apart of "the organic impulse" has been observed in *Death of a Salesman* with its concluding "Requiem." Moreover, Miller has also been seen to depart from the second of his two basic principles of playwriting in introducing narrative and expository passages into *The Crucible*. With *A View from the Bridge* he wrote a play that approaches illustrated narrative.

Alfieri, the lawyer-narrator, opens the play by telling a little about himself and his neighborhood and suggesting some of the themes of the play to follow. When Eddie appears on the stage, the verbal tense Alfieri makes use of is striking in its implications: "This one's name *was* Eddie Carbone" [my italics]. Later in the play Alfieri consistently refers to Eddie in the past tense. The story is obviously Alfieri's story. What we see on the stage is Alfieri's memory of Eddie as he ponders on its significance: "This is the end of the story. Good night," he concludes the original one-act version of the play. The past tense is the mode of narrative; drama is enacted in the present.

The title *A Memory of Two Mondays* is in itself interesting in this connection as it suggests an implied narrator, someone whose memory is projected on the stage as is Alfieri's. This technique is developed to its furthest extreme in *After the Fall*, where *"the action takes place in the mind, thought, and memory of Quentin."* The play has become illustrated narrative, and is essentially a two-act monologue which the narrator and main character Quentin, directs at the audience. Significantly, since the flow of narration is essential to the play and the many dramatizations of situations in the narrative are incidental, Quentin's audience is in Miller's stage directions defined as a *"Listener, who, if he could be seen, would be sitting just beyond the edge of the stage itself."*

The images presented on the stage are illustrations of Quentin's consciously controlled discourse or of the working of his sub-consciousness as he struggles for self-understanding and self-acceptance. In either case, the device of giving characters within *"the mind, thought, and memory of Quentin"* a semi-independent status on the stage and allowing them to speak for themselves, makes possible an objective view of the self-image projected by Quentin in his discourse. Essentially, however, Miller has placed a character on the stage and given him the opportunity of examining his life and motives and explaining himself to a Listener through a monologue that lasts the whole length of a two-act play. From point of view of genre the result is a cross between expressionist drama, stream-of-consciousness novel and dramatic monologue. The result, however, is good theater: it works on the stage. The critical attacks on *After the Fall* have mainly been concerned with Miller's subject matter and theme, not his experiment with dramatic form.

Rather than add a clarifying "Requiem," as he did with *Death of a Salesman;* rather than interpolate expository passages in the published play to make himself more readily understood, as he did in *The Crucible;* and rather than introduce a narrator, somewhat to the side of the central plot, who could explain the author's "reading of its significance," Miller in *After the Fall* made the narrator's attempt to arrive at the significance of his own life and explain himself directly to the audience the center of the play. Ironically, Miller may never have felt himself so misunderstood by audiences and critics alike as after the first production of *After the Fall* in 1964, the play that may be seen as the culmination of a series of efforts to develop a form that would allow him to present his intentions unmistakably and clearly to his public.

Some years earlier, in his introduction to the *Collected Plays,* Miller had observed that "the intention behind a work of art and its effects upon the public are not always the same." His answers to the question of how to avoid this communication gap could not, finally, have struck him as successful in practice. In his next play, at least, *Incident at Vichy,* written immediately after the critical disaster of *After the Fall,* he returned to the form of the straightforward, realistic play. By concentrating on one of the two poorly integrated themes of *After the Fall,* that represented by the concentration camp tower, the later play, moreover, avoids the conflict between two different kinds of "morality" or "motivation" many critics have found in his plays up to and including *After the Fall. Incident at Vichy* may be too much the drama of ideas (and not very new or original ones at that) to be successful in the theater, and Von Berg's development may not be quite convincing on the stage; but at least there is no need for any "Requiem," explanatory footnotes or narrator to express the play's dominantly public theme.

Four years later Miller returned to the material of *All My Sons, Death of a Salesman* and *After the Fall* in another family drama, *The Price.* The play is also a return to the realistic style and retrospective technique of *All My Sons.* But of course Miller had traveled a long distance since 1947. There is greater economy of characters and incidents, a more subtle and dramatically integrated use of symbols, no more need for manipulative, mechanistic devices like surprise arrivals or unsuspected letters. Two hours in an attic with old furniture and four people—and the experience in the theater is of something organic, something that comes alive and evolves before us on the stage. The playwright appears relaxed, confident that the "action" expresses its "generalized significance": the characters speak for themselves and the play speaks for Arthur Miller.

The critics who found, I think rightly so, a confusion of private-psychological and public-political themes in Miller's plays were addressing themselves to the very problem Miller has repeatedly pointed to as the central one for the dramatist in our day: how to create a form that can bridge "the deep split between the private life of man and his social life." Miller's belief, expressed in several essays in the mid-fifties, that it is the unrealistic modes of drama that are capable of expressing man's social relationships, as opposed to the realistic drama which is best suited to present the private life, is seen most clearly at work in *A View from the Bridge* from 1955. The "bridge," however, is rather crudely built: to the side of the realistic action stands the narrator, who in the first version of the play spoke in verse—poetry, according to Miller, being the style most closely related to public themes. In the light of such theories the author's misfired intentions with *After the Fall,* his most "unrealistic" play, may be more easily understood; and the irony of its reception as his most embarrassingly private play more readily appreciated. There is further irony in the success-ful synthesis of the public and the private spheres in *The Price.* For accord-ing to Miller's theory, the realism of this or any other play "could not, with ease and beauty, bridge the widening gap between the private life and the social life." But in this essay on "The Family in Modern Drama," Miller had also wondered: "Why does Realism always seem to be drawing us all back to its arms? We have not yet created in this country a succinct form to take its place." This was written at a time when Miller was trying to break away from realism. This movement, however, had its temporary conclusion in *After the Fall,* the play that more than any other must have led Miller to despair of communicating his intentions to his audience.

The ironies of Arthur Miller's career as a dramatist were further com-pounded with the production of *The Creation of the World and Other Business* in 1973. In spite of the success, with audiences as well as with critics, of *The Price,* following the disastrous reception of his experiments in *After the Fall,* Miller seems unable to rest comfortably in the strong and protective arms of Realism. His latest play is his first attempt to express himself through comedy and pure fantasy, and in this his most radical departure from realism his earlier concern with the problems of integrating man's private and social life has given way to teleological speculation. Be-hind the fanciful cosmological draperies, however, one may discover the playwright's old story of the two sons and familial conflict. Indeed, the new play serves as a reminder that the Cain and Abel story is an archetypal pattern in *All My Sons, Death of a Salesman, After the Fall* and *The Price*.

In a different guise the old question of the two centers of interest is also raised by Miller's attempt at comedy. While God and Lucifer incessantly come together on the stage to discuss the Creator's design, Miller's alleged theme, the audience, who cannot but grow restless after two acts with God, his Angels and a boring couple named Adam and Eve, are finally given the two sons, the responsible and respected Cain and the irresponsible and loved Abel. The rather simplistic psychological presentation of the conflict between them is the kind of dramatic material Miller has successfully handled before, and both because it is welcome relief from the overall tediousness of the rest of the play and because it has dramatic potential, it will easily lay claim to the attention and the interest of the audience at the expense of the play's concern with the human dilemma. Miller's latest Broadway venture thus is not only thematically related to his first one but shows that the playwright has still not been able to solve the problem of dramatic form he then felt had served to obscure his main theme.

The story of Arthur Miller's struggle with dramatic form had its beginning in his realization of the two centers of interest in *All My Sons*. His subsequent theories of social drama and its relationship to the realistic and unrealistic modes of drama should be regarded primarily as rationalizations of his own attempts to express himself clearly, to bridge the gap not so much between the social and the private as between his conscious intentions and the audience and critical responses. This was fully demonstrated in his attempts deliberately to separate the action of a play from its significance. His distrust of the realistic drama as a usable medium was thus properly a distrust of the theater itself as a medium, as evidenced in his use of intermediary commentary and narrators and in his tendency towards illustrated narrative. Realism nevertheless has proved to have a strong hold on Miller, and it is the mode with which, the evidence of his plays suggests, he is most at home. *The Creation of the World and Other Business* marks a break with the tone and style of all his previous plays, but it is impossible at this point to guess whether it will turn out to be a new departure in his career or a dead end. Although Miller, like the devil in Ibsen's *Peer Gynt,* has not always been able to reckon with his audience, he has demonstrated that he has been extremely sensitive to their responses. He may therefore accept the common verdict of critics and audiences and return to the kind of work that has placed him in the front rank of contemporary dramatists.

DENNIS WELLAND

The Drama of Forgiveness

T*he Inside of His Head* would have made a better alternative title for
After the Fall than for *Death of a Salesman*. The dramatic form Miller
evolved for the later play is dictated by this concept and suggests how
Death of a Salesman might have been constructed had Miller believed the
theatre in 1949 (or even perhaps himself as a playwright) to have been
ready for it. More fluid than its predecessor, its easier fluctuations in time,
place and mood enable it to take on more issues and more widely-ranging
ones, public as well as private. The fifteen years between the two plays
had enriched Miller's experience and his skill as a dramatist; most of the
themes in *After the Fall* had preoccupied him in earlier works and seemed
now to be brought together for a mature reexamination of their interacting
complexities.

For all its apparent adventurousness, however, the fluidity of form
works against it. The scenes of recall in *Death of a Salesman*, involving as
they do a change of acting area, sometimes changes of costume, sometimes
the introduction of a few properties, acquire the status of inset episodes;
they have a duration and an identity that make a sharper theatrical impact
than the more fragmented, kaleidoscopic glimpses of the past in *After the
Fall*. The demonstrable sequence in which they recur, being dictated by
Willy's subconscious, determines more clearly the structure and thrust of
the play, affording an ordered and progressive disclosure of his personal
guilt and responsibility for what has happened. This, together with the sense

From *Arthur Miller: A Study of His Plays.* ©1979 by Dennis Welland. Methuen and
Co. Ltd., 1979.

of an ongoing dramatic action not yet concluded, sustains the element of surprise and thus the audience's interest.

The form of *After the Fall* is essentially the dramatic monologue interspersed by representations of past events, and in the theatre this is no real substitute for dramatic action. That Quentin is on stage throughout, speaking directly to the audience, might seem to place him more fully in control than Willy of the re-presentation of the past but in fact it emphasises the static nature of the play. In the cinema "voice-over" techniques could keep Quentin-in-the-present in the audience's mind's eye less obtrusively; on stage he is too literally in their vision. This and the fact that he has already accepted, more fully and more consciously than Willy, the extent of his personal guilt for the past, puts the play at the disadvantage of seeming only to rehash a sequence of events already concluded. Dramatic *tour de force* that the role of Quentin indisputably is, it nevertheless imposes on the character a passivity and a completedness that Willy, though the lesser man, does not have in the theatre.

A "stream of consciousness" play in a sense that *Death of a Salesman* is not, *After the Fall* relies, with greater sophistication, on an associational process of recall more real in its seeming inconsequentiality than Willy's. Psychologically it is thus less "artificial" but, *pace* much modern experimentation, the theatre itself *is* artificial and plays *are* artifacts. Acceptance of this does not force all drama into outworn and stereotyped moulds, but it may help to concentrate the playwright's mind on what is feasible and effective on the stage.

One critic in 1965 saw this new play as a failure because it "remains a realistic play with scenes rearranged in time and space." It is more genuinely experimental than that, but what he calls "Miller's unquenchable devotion to realism" seems to me to create one problem. To suggest a world external to his characters Miller uses non-speaking extras who pass across the stage or materialise in momentary tableaux. There are more than two dozen of these, together with three or four characters who, though named, have only one line or so to deliver. Not only is this uneconomical but it may too easily confuse the audience, who will inevitably expect some at least of these walking-on characters to make a larger contribution to the continuing story line than in fact they do. It may also be questioned whether such background figures would really feature in Quentin's stream of consciousness and thus whether their introduction is not superfluous and the result of a mixture of methods.

This play was, of course, commissioned as the opening production at the new Lincoln Center for the Performing Arts in New York City. Such occasions encourage the display of the theatre's flexibility and adaptability in ways to which the conventional proscenium-arch, "fourth-wall-removed" kind of play lends itself less readily, and at least one critic commended the original production for moving "like mist over the platforms and parapets of the big, open acting area. . . . There is no picture-frame stage, no curtain, no scenery, no teasers to hide lights. It is a theater of revealment for a drama of revealment." The sets were designed by Jo Mielziner who had designed the original *Death of a Salesman*; Elia Kazan, who had directed that play but not worked with Miller since, directed *After the Fall*.

The play has grandness of conception and boldness of design: the role of Quentin is a virtuoso piece of writing which produced a widely-acclaimed performance from Jason Robards. *The Saturday Evening Post* announced enthusiastically that "he joins in active dialogue for three solid hours, an even longer role than Hamlet's." Others, however, were quick to condemn the scale of the play as reflecting self-indulgence on the author's part rather than artistic greatness.

II

The *Post's* comment accompanied its publication of the complete text of this "powerful drama" within a week of the opening which it hailed as a "national experience." In a specially-written foreword Miller dwelt characteristically on the large moral implications of a play that he defined as "the trial of a man by his own conscience, his own values, his own deeds." Admittedly the cover featured Barbara Loden, the actress who created the role of Maggie, as a "sensational new find" and referred to Miller's "hottest new play since *Death of a Salesman*," but in no other respect did the *Post's* presentation impute to the play any sensationalism.

Three weeks later *Life International* announced on its cover: "Marilyn's Ghost. Arthur Miller writes about his shocking new play." Inside, Tom Prideaux, after the tribute (already quoted) to "a drama of revealment," asked pointedly whether too much was revealed and decided that "Quentin protests too much" in the "kind of moral strip-tease" that he performs, especially in the first half of the play. "The second half," he declared "takes fire as it focuses sharply on Maggie." Identifying her with Marilyn Monroe, he exonerated Miller from the charge of "serious bad taste" that was being brought against him, and praised instead his courage in telling "the truth, as he saw it, against himself."

Miller's own one-page article which followed was entitled "With respect for her agony—but with love." It expressed surprise at the outcry, which he saw as hypocritical, of people who charged him with "cruelty toward the memory of Marilyn Monroe" and denied that Maggie is a representation of Marilyn: she is only "a character in a play about the human animal's unwillingness or inability to discover in himself the seeds of his own destruction." Again he shifts the argument, with dignity as well as deftness, on to a higher and wider moral plane, but he does it much more defensively than in the rather Olympian foreword in the *Post*. The debate that was to bedevil so much discussion of this play had begun. As Prideaux observed, however much Miller repeated that Maggie was not the real Marilyn, "the play itself invites the comparison—not invites, insists on, really." W. J. Weatherby points out that not only was Barbara Loden made to look as much like Marilyn as possible, but at least one incident is taken straight from Marilyn's life: "she had had an affair with a leading Hollywood agent who was married and whose family excluded her when he died even though his last words were about her." That, in Maggie's account of this, the agent should have been transformed into a judge requires some modification of my earlier comments on the high esteem in which Miller usually holds lawyers, but it does not diminish the significance of his inclusion of the incident. As Weatherby says, "There are too many incidents and remarks that recall the Miller-Monroe relationship for the play not to seem a revelation of what went on behind the scenes and to be Miller's view of what went wrong. . . . But many admirers of hers were indignant at the portrait and the interpretation." All in all, it was obviously ingenuous of Miller to express the hope that, within the foreseeable future, the play can be separated from "Marilyn's golden image."

What was largely at issue, of course, was the tarnishing of that image. The golden girl of *The Misfits*, whose insecurity had ripened into love, had been supplanted by this drug-addicted neurotic whose insecurity had extinguished love, and in whom the fey, trusting innocence of Roslyn had given way to moral irresponsibility, egotistic and unfeeling arrogance, and a vulgar viciousness. Weatherby speaks of Maggie as "the other side of Roslyn . . . the missing side that made her unsatisfying in the movie and hard for Monroe to make convincing," but to many people it looked as though, in Maggie, Miller had portrayed too emphatically the "monster" that Marilyn had accused him of being unable to accept in her. People do not take kindly to the destruction of their myths, nor, indeed to the insistence that they *are* myths. Here, in their indignation, they blamed Miller for the destruction of something when he was in reality trying to show them that, if it had ever existed at all, it had in fact destroyed itself. Quentin/Miller is agonising over his own inability to arrest that process, and even questioning whether it was not, perhaps, unwillingness as much as inability; this however, moved the audience less (understandably) than the recentness of the painful events he was dramatising. The rawness of Maggie/Marilyn's agony was more apparent to them than the respect and love which Miller claimed had prompted him to the depiction of it. The relationship between Quentin and Maggie culminates with dramatic appropriateness in this realisation: "Maggie, we were both born of many errors; a human being has to forgive himself! Neither of us is innocent. What more do you want?" Fearful that he himself cannot love, he tries to force from her the admission "And I am full of hatred; I, Maggie, sweet lover of all life—I hate the world!" Looked at dispassionately this says, about their respective responsibilities for the break-up, little more than Marilyn Monroe had already admitted privately to W. J. Weatherby. Reviewing the opening performance in *The New York Times* as "a pain-wracked drama . . . Mr. Miller's maturest," Howard Taubman rightly insisted that "it seeks to understand, not to judge." Accepting this, many people still felt uncomfortably voyeuristic at being involved in the process, and their inability successfully to disengage Maggie from Marilyn (especially when Barbara Loden's appearance so strongly resembled that of the dead star) should not have surprised Miller as totally as it seems to have done.

III

Yet even if the passage of time has blunted sensibilities on this score, the structure of *After the Fall* still confronts us with critical problems. So compelling in its intensity is the treatment of Maggie that, as Tom Prideaux pointed out, the second part of the play does indeed take fire in its concentration on that theme. The first part by contrast, is less clear in its thrust, more uneasy in its movement. Before it has opened the Maggie theme, the first part has tried to encompass Quentin's relationship with his parents and brother, his first wife Louise, two mistresses (Felice and Elsie), as well as his friends Lou (Elsie's husband) and Mickey, with whom he shares a past involvement in left-wing politics; it also introduces his developing relationship with the German girl Holga and his sense of involvement, through her, in the anti-Semitism of the Nazi concentration camps.

It is questionable whether the fragmented episodic stream-of-consciousness method is really adequate in the establishment of so many and such varied themes. Are *both* Felice and Elsie essential? Is the political theme sufficiently developed? That Lou's suicide should relieve Quentin of the necessity for a painful moral decision is, like Maggie's suicide, in line with the play's recurrent suggestion that Quentin is in some ways the man who had all the luck—his problems are removed before he has to solve them—but the guilt is the more oppressive because of that. Nevertheless, Lou's suicide tends to look more like a trick of dramatic convenience, and Mickey's disappearance from the play unfortunately reinforces this impression. What is no doubt a conscientious attempt to keep this one theme in proportion to the others begins to look unfortunately like an evasion of it. By making Quentin a lawyer by profession Miller may intend a secularisation of the Catholic adage *corruptio optimi est pessima*: that the wisdom, firmness of judgment, and moral rightness associated with that profession in the earlier plays are not evident here could constitute a significant indictment of the perturbed times, but although Quentin agonises over Lou and Mickey he never seems as professionally involved with the issue as one would have expected Miller to make him.

Moreover, to counterpoint Quentin's lack of involvement there with his growing interest in Maggie is unfortunately to belittle both. Quentin forgets to attend the meeting of his colleagues specially convened to discuss his and the firm's future if he persists in the defence of Lou; his forgetfulness is occasioned, in the action of the play, by his first chance meeting with Maggie in the park, and is subsequently rationalised by Louise as a manifestation of unconscious fear. Yet neither of these, nor even the combination of them, carries quite enough credibility. What sort of a lawyer, already divided between loyalty to a friend and professional self-interest, allows the issue to be driven so casually out of his mind? Whatever fascination Maggie exudes, and however emotionally upset Quentin already is, could such an infatuation take him so quickly and so completely "out of this world"?

His dilemma over whether or not to defend Lou is at once complicated and simplified by two other elements that merit closer scrutiny than Miller allows him to give them. One is Lou's admission that, in the original book on the revision of which he is now working, he had deliberately suppressed evidence unfavourable to the Communist cause. Of course, as the play is concerned with Quentin's discovery that no one can be as innocent as he has believed them to be, some imperfection in Lou has to be demonstrated. However, Lou's fear of "being forced to defend my own incredible lies" leaves ambiguous the extent to which the new book will actually repudiate the old; Mickey attributes the lies in the earlier version to Elsie's influence more than to Lou's dedication to the cause; and Elsie's impassioned hostility to the publication of the new book may be ascribed to any of several causes unspecified in the text. Quentin's readiness to judge others is reiterated by several characters in the play, including himself, yet on all these issues he takes no steps to satisfy himself and passes no explicit judgment. Psychologically explicable as this may be, dramatically it requires more clarification than Miller gives it. The reluctance to pose the matter in terms too sharply black and white is characteristic of him and commendable, but it leads to an obfuscation difficult to penetrate in print and almost impossible in the theatre. That Lou's wife, Elsie, is yet another woman to whom Quentin is sexually attracted is again consistent with Quentin's extramarital adventurousness, but its implications for Quentin's attitude to the defence of Lou are insufficiently explored. It is for reasons such as these that Lou's suicide seems contrived to let Miller off the dramatic hook as much as to let Quentin off the moral one.

More strikingly, however, than any other of his plays, *After the Fall* polarises differences of critical response, and at least one commentator describes the first half of the play as "a towering achievement":

> The form unfolds as the mind touches various events revealing decisive details of Quentin's life and asking the audience to be concerned with the limits of love, the response of the beloved, the meaning of friendship, justice, truth. Miller imposes no specific dogma, but asks for common speculation into mutual concerns.

This assumes that the play will necessarily stimulate the concern for which it asks, and, like the play itself, it assumes concern to be an adequate form of audience-involvement. Harsh as it is to say so, Quentin is concerned with all these issues, and he has feelings about them that do him credit; for a lawyer, he may seem to many laymen to be guided far too quickly by his emotions and his concern, far too little by the intellect on which his professional success has presumably depended. The theatre is not a debating chamber, but the audience's concern might be more readily engaged and developed into a constructive interest if Quentin's concern were more convincingly seen to be the rational product of self-analysis and a growing understanding of his predicament.

The associated themes of Holga and the concentration camps also seem to me posited rather than developed and integrated with the rest. We need to be sure that Holga is not merely the latest in the succession of women in whom Quentin has pinned his faith, and that the experiences he has undergone really have developed in Quentin a capacity for love. These things are implied but are they established? Is it an economy of dramatic method or a cutting of dramatic corners?

The play begins and ends with Quentin saying "Hello!" The first

"Hello!" is a natural, unobtrusive greeting of the unseen interlocutor represented by the audience; the final "Hello!" is in reply to Holga's and the exchange is clearly intended to signal a new beginning, as does his upward movement towards her through the ranks of the other characters with whom he has presumably come finally to terms. (If the final stage-direction reference to them as "endlessly alive" is intended in any way to qualify this impression it is hard to see how it could be realised on the stage.) The significance of the "Hello!" is underlined further by the division between the two acts. The first act ends, apart from a two-line exchange between Quentin and Maggie, with Quentin telling the "Listener": "I'd like to settle this. Although actually I (*laughs*) only came to say hello"; the second opens with Holga greeting him warmly, "Quentin! Here! Hello! Hello!"

A similar underlining is effected by another recurrent phrase. At the end of Quentin's long opening speech after the initial "Hello!" he tells the "Listener": "The truth is that every morning when I awake, I'm full of hope! . . . I open my eyes, I'm like a boy!" At the end of the act he repeats it: "I open up my eyes each morning like a boy, even now." At the end of the play Holga "materialises" for the last time, repeating her phrase, "But no one is innocent they did not kill!" and then bidding him "Hello!"; Quentin responds to her hope by reiterating, "And that, that's why I wake each morning like a boy—even now, even now! I swear to you, I could love the world again!" The process by which the regained faith is conveyed to us is discernible and effective; the process by which it has been achieved would have been clearer if the action had allowed a fuller development of Holga as a character and not merely an inspiration. This in turn might have made the concentration camp theme something more than the rather facile symbol of a wider guilt that it sometimes seems.

IV

These strictures are in no way intended to impugn Miller's sincerity and depth of feeling nor to minimise the reality of the psychological and moral insights he has brought to it. What the play says is both pertinent and admirable, but in the theatre are its themes of guilt and moral responsibility sufficiently articulated dramatically as distinct from verbally? However acceptable its "philosophy" may be, it must be conveyed by the play as a whole and not merely by homiletic speeches. That "the action takes place in the mind, thought, and memory of Quentin" does not exonerate the playwright from the duty of providing a dramatic action that is seen to have a unity in the Aristotelian and not merely the psychologically-subjective sense.

For Quentin as for Willy Loman, images arise from the family past to torment him. Two of these revive the "two brothers" pattern: the simpler is the memory of the childhood incident when the parents took his elder brother Dan to Atlantic City, sending Quentin for a walk with the maid to avoid having to take him too. The toy sailing boat they bring him back is no compensation for the sense of betrayal which, he later decides, is "the only truth that sticks." It seems to have been one of the rare occasions when he did not get what he wanted, for the second memory is of his having been given the opportunity of a college education by Dan's self-sacrifice in staying at home to support their father. Quentin's guilt at this surfaces in the play when he recalls his father's reproach: "What you *want!* Always what you *want!* Chris-sake, *what are you!"*

These incidents, together with Quentin's third and most haunting memory of his father's ruin in the Depression of the 1930s, are grafted neatly into the action of *After the Fall*, most of them in act 2. The sailboat memory first occurs, with appropriate irony, when he accuses himself of trying to love everybody: it reminds him of his inability to mourn his mother and modulates into his inability to mourn Maggie. The college memory occurs when Holga's fear that "I may not be all that interesting" is contrasted with Louise's assertion "I am not all this uninteresting, Quentin!": he contemplates leaving Holga as he has left Louise ("there *is* some freedom in the going") only to recall how his mother, who idolised him as a child, encouraged him in what he now sees as the treason of deserting his father in order to pursue his own ambition. Dan's promise to "send you a list of books to read" dissolves neatly into another time as Maggie immediately asks in reply, "But could I read them?"

The most traumatic of these experiences is introduced even more skilfully at a much earlier stage of the play and is developed into a more extended scene. Triggered off by his visit with Holga to the concentration camp, it comes so unexpectedly as to force from him the question "But what the hell has this got to do with a concentration camp?" To some extent he has anticipated this in his previous speech, when he recognises his inability to weep as Holga can at "this slaughterhouse" with which he feels an understanding, and when he links this with his inability to mourn his mother. (The only "family recall" scene to precede this has been of breaking to his father the news of the mother's death and realising that he himself does not "seem to know how to grieve for her.") The scene begins deceptively on a note of comedy: Quentin as a child is being smartened up to attend his uncle's wedding, and his mother's meandering monologue ranges over the inadequacies of his handwriting, speech and posture, her brother's capacity to make every wedding in the family a catastrophe, and her husband's absence from the last such occasion through falling asleep in a Turkish bath. Pride in her husband's personality clashes with memories of his earlier illiteracy and of the college career she sacrificed to marry him; at the same time she recalls sentimentally the penniless medical student her father had injudiciously forbidden her to marry ("Who knew he'd end up so big in the gallstones?" she asks rhetorically). This promising vein of Jewish humour is exploited further when her husband assures her he has not forgotten the wedding: "I wish I could, but I'm paying for it . . . They all fall in love on my money. I married into a love nest!" Then, with appalling suddenness, it is sabotaged by the phone conversation to which, uncomprehendingly, she listens as he discovers that he is bankrupt. The cross-examination by which she establishes the full extent of the disaster rises from incredulity to vituperation and contemptuous abuse culminating in a final estranging insult "You are an idiot!"

A beautifully managed, though painful, scene in its own right, it also exhibits Miller's stagecraft by its dramatic release of what is to be a key word throughout the play. In vain does the mother, a moment later, deny to Quentin that she has insulted his father ("Well, I was a little angry, that's all, but I never said *that*. I think he's a wonderful man!"): she compounds the cruelty by the well-meant deceit, and the treachery is unforgettable. At crisis after crisis Quentin will remember his mother uttering the one word "Idiot!" Yet the fact that the word, or a derivative of it, occurs at least fourteen times in the play and is only on four of these associated specifically with his mother's use of it illustrates the firmness with which Miller implants it in our consciousness and the effectiveness with which he draws on the association. Elsie's reiterated "He's a moral idiot!" is deliberately ambiguous in its application: she may mean Mickey, she may mean her husband, she may even mean Quentin, and since Quentin remembering her use of the phrase always remembers her drawing her bathrobe across her as she says it, he obviously regards it as an exclusion of him from the intimacy that the falling open of her robe has first occasioned between them.

One powerful recurrence of the word shows how deeply it has seared into Quentin's mind. It occurs when he is desperately trying to force Maggie into an admission of her own responsibility for what is happening to them. "If you could only say," he tells her, " 'I have been cruel,' this frightening room would open. If you could say, 'I have been kicked around, but I have been just as inexcusably vicious to others, called my husband idiot in public.' " Now on the evidence of the text, this is something that Maggie has *not* done. Louise has, but only in private, Elsie may have, but Maggie has

not. Yet to Quentin, convinced as he is of Maggie's turpitude, it is inconceivable that she should not have been guilty, like his mother, of this pecu-
liarly heinous act of treachery. Even in this "drama of revealment" this
instinctive transfer of the mother's guilt to the wife is outstanding as a
revelation of Quentin's state of mental distress: it is a masterly touch but it
may be too subtle to make in the theatre the full impact that it should.

Counterpointing this savage melody of "idiot," however, is another,
more tender one that is introduced almost as soon as the original clash
between Quentin's parents has dissolved back to the concentration camp.
Holga, whose hopefulness Quentin admires, tells him, "I think it's a mistake
to ever look for hope outside one's self" and goes on to describe a recurring
dream that she has experienced:

> I dreamed I had a child, and even in the dream I saw it was my
> life, and it was an idiot, and I ran away. But it always crept on
> to my lap again, clutched at my clothes. Until I thought, if I could
> kiss it, whatever in it was my own, perhaps I could sleep. And I
> bent to its broken face, and it was horrible . . . but I kissed it. I
> think one must finally take one's life in one's arms, Quentin.

Parabolically it embodies the "message" of the play, perhaps a little too
sententiously, but there is real skill in this linking of the two themes: acceptance of the idiot child exorcises the "Idiot!" The play has some way to
go before Quentin learns this lesson, but the "idiot child" image haunts him,
and Quentin, when he does something that he regrets, almost always speaks
of it as "idiotic," thus ambivalently evoking both motifs.

V

By another dextrous piece of counterpointing Quentin's response to
this speech of Holga's releases a word that is a useful key to another of the
play's main themes. Fumblingly, all he can say is, "It sounds foolish, but I
feel . . . unblessed." As he does so, he momentarily visualises Felice as a
reminder to himself and to the audience that in one respect he is embarrassed to be as blessed as he is. "I'll always bless you. Always!" Felice has
told him on her first appearance, and this time too, though she does not
speak, she "holds up her hand in blessing." Whenever she is recalled it is in
association with this single act. At the very end of the play Felice is again
automatically about to raise her arm in blessing when "he shakes her hand,
aborting her enslavement." There is an ambiguity here: is it her enslavement
of him by her perpetual benediction that is being aborted, or is he freeing

her from her enslavement *to* him? In the theatre the distinction is unimportant: the silent gesture merely terminates a relationship. The stage direction has, however, implications that merit discussion, for either interpretation or both can be supported from the text. Quentin has already admitted to us "there's something about that girl unnerves me . . . And she meant so little to me. I feel like a mirror in which she saw herself as glorious." Yet the memory of her recurs time and again, enslaving him to the guilt it evokes. The confidence and the self-respect Felice has derived from her relationship with him are, of course, precisely what he gives initially to Maggie. Inevitably the two are later recalled in this context simultaneously and Quentin recognises that "there is a fraud involved; I have no such power." Felice's attitude remains constant and he cannot bear it: "It frightens me, and I wish to God she'd stop blessing me!"

Felice's sole function in the play is thus to epitomise for us Quentin's capacity to inspire in others a confidence and a love that he is unable adequately to reciprocate. She, alone of his four "pre-Holga" women, sustains her love for him despite this and can always bless him: perhaps because of this she is dramatically the least realised of all of them. The phrase that she uses to convey her affection has other resonances, though. "I bless you, girl," Gay told Roslyn, and it is the nearest Miller allows himself to go in implying a happy ending to *The Misfits*. "I bless you, Quentin!" says Maggie in the second act of this play, and it is linked in his memory with his mother blessing him earlier. "God bless this child," says the black servant Carrie at Maggie's wedding: it is the only specific mention of God in conjunction with what is elsewhere consistently an expression of affection. "I bless you" may well be another of those phrases of Miller's that has a Jewish origin, but its force in this play is unmistakable. The nearest Quentin comes to it is significant: "Holga, I bless your uncertainty. You don't seem to be looking for some goddamned . . . moral *victory*." By the end of the play such victory as he has achieved may seem singularly Pyrrhic, but what he has learnt could, not inappropriately, be formulated in W. H. Auden's lines, "And life remains a blessing / Although you cannot bless."

Quentin's final speech, expressing tentatively such conclusions as he has reached, is, in its hesitant eloquence, as fine as any Miller has written. It brings together the dominant themes of the play melodically in a *reprise* of the key phrases and ideas:

> What burning cities taught her and the death of love taught me
> . . . that's why I woke each morning like a boy . . . To know, and
> even happily, that we meet unblessed . . . after the Fall . . . Is the

knowing all? And the wish to kill is never killed, but with some gift of courage one may look into its face when it appears, and with a stroke of love—as to an idiot in the house—forgive it.

The most humane of all Miller's plays up to this point, *After the Fall* is ultimately concerned with forgiveness, but not in a sentimental way. Ironically, had it been more sentimental, less candid in its analysis of Maggie, it would have occasioned less hostility and been more readily judged on dramatic than on moral grounds. It would still not have been one of his best plays in the theatre: it lacks *The Crucible*'s simple directness of dramatic line and *Death of a Salesman*'s newness of dramatic idiom; the dilemma of its protagonist is more specialised and personal. Yet, like all of Miller's plays, it is a gloss on the idea expressed by Meredith:

> In tragic life, God wot,
> No villain need be; passion spins the plot:
> We are betrayed by what is false within.

Quietly but firmly, however, it denies the possibility of apportioning the blame to outside forces that is still as available to Willy Loman's sympathisers as it was to Willy.

After the Fall, for all its faults, merits respect greater than is sometimes accorded it and closer critical attention than is possible in the theatre. Its text can reveal to the student a carefully-patterned structure and an integrity of approach to which, in the future, when the rawness of feeling about Marilyn Monroe has tempered more with the passing of time, a revival may be able to do more justice on the stage.

LEONARD MOSS

The Perspective of a Playwright

I. THESIS

Arthur Miller has focused upon a single subject—"the struggle . . . of the individual attempting to gain his 'rightful' position in his society" and in his family. Miller's chief characters, whether they eventually revise their objectives or remain rigidly defensive, are motivated by an obsession to justify themselves; they fix their identities through radical acts of ego-assertion. "However one might dislike this man, who does all sorts of frightful things," the dramatist comments of Eddie Carbone [in his *Collected Plays*], "he possesses or exemplifies the wondrous and humane fact that he too can be driven to what in the last analysis is a sacrifice of himself for his conception, however misguided, of right, dignity, and justice." High rank or noble status does not distinguish such figures. "The commonest of men," Miller states in "Tragedy and the Common Man" (1949), "may take on [tragic] stature to the extent of his willingness to throw all he has into the contest." "The closer a man approaches tragedy the more intense is his concentration of emotion upon the fixed point of his commitment, which is to say the closer he approaches what in life we call fanaticism."

Fanatical self-assertion may bring an individual into violent opposition with his society. Tragic antagonism arises because the "unchangeable [social] environment" often "suppresses man, perverts the flowing out of his love and creative instinct" ("Tragedy and the Common Man"). According to Miller, in "The Shadows of the Gods" (1958), conflict between father and son prefigures tragedy's "revolutionary questioning" when the child

From *Arthur Miller*. © 1980 by Twayne Publishers, a division of G. K. Hall & Co., Inc.

affirms his independence after confronting an intolerant parental authority. Later the mature hero, in life and in art, directs his protest against restrictive forces more potent than the father's, for "in truth the parent, powerful as he appears, is not the source of injustice but its deputy."

Society, however, is not the sole tragic villain. Miller admires his hero's obsessive claim to a given "right," and he sorrows at its frustration. At the same time, he realizes that total self-concern can lead to total self-defeat; "conscience," if not tempered by humility and informed by reason, may degenerate into a savagely destructive faculty. When opposed by "forces of disintegration," Miller's major figures react in either of two ways, depending upon the flexibility of their ethical posture. They may reexamine their criteria, as in the case of David Frieber, Lawrence Newman, Chris Keller, Biff Loman, John Proctor, Gay Langland, Quentin, Prince Von Berg, and Victor Franz. Or they may persist in their assertion even though persistence brings catastrophe to themselves and to those for whom they care. That is the course chosen by Joe Keller, Willy Loman, Eddie Carbone, Maggie, and Cain, each of whom arrives at "the end of his justifications." In the first instance, accommodation is directed by realistic self-knowledge; in the second, "constancy" to an ideal of self-love remains the paramount value. The fanatic rejects "truth," which he fears will undermine his "power," alienate him from others, and negate his longing for "respect" and "peace." Despite the nagging pressure of guilt-feelings, he commits the grossest acts, even suicide, in order to maintain the sanctity of his "name"—pride in his adequacy as a father or lover, citizen or businessman—and to prevent the exposure of his secret weakness, dependence, malice, or shame. "To perceive somehow our own complicity with evil is a horror not to be borne."

The author's moral bias is clearly evident in these divergent reactions. Individuals can buttress their own and society's stability by resisting "hatred" and "exclusiveness." Or individuals can upset social equilibrium by enforcing the exaggerated demands of a narrow egoism. Lawrence Newman and John Proctor (among others) strengthen their communities even though they defy popular standards; Willy Loman and Joe Keller adopt popular standards but become estranged from both family and society because of their uncompromising self-will. Extreme egocentrism inevitably thwarts a man's constructive energies: the only way to acquire dignity is to respect the dignity of others.

Miller has proposed his version of the Golden Rule in many essays. He has denounced writers who conform to commercial specifications, businessmen and politicians who exploit other men's insecurities, informers who betray friends in order to preserve their own reputations, civilians who passively tolerate wartime atrocities, and veterans who quickly forget the comradeship they knew during combat. He encountered the last while gathering material in American army camps for a movie. In his journal of the tour, *Situation Normal* (1944), he reports that soldiers, after sharing a common purpose in battle, lose their "unity of feeling" on returning to the United States: "civilian life in America is private, it is always striving for exclusiveness."

Whatever the specific situation, his point on the necessity for communication between individuals and their institutional sources of value remains the same. He repeatedly stresses the idea that the proper business of serious drama is to demonstrate the feasibility of such communication and the disastrous results of its absence. The protagonist of this drama must enter into meaningful social relationships, if only to challenge conventional norms. He should possess "the worth, the innate dignity, of a whole people asking a basic question and demanding its answer" ("On Social Plays," 1955). The "identity" he molds within the intimate bonds of his family must be tried in an inhospitable world. Society as a whole, Miller explains in "The Family in Modern Drama" (1956), is "mutable, accidental, and consequently of a profoundly arbitrary nature to us." A limited theater will therefore restrict its scope to the family, which symbolizes what is "real" and abiding in human affairs. But a writer "cannot hope to achieve truly high excellence short of an investigation into the whole gamut of causation of which society is a manifest and crucial part." He must answer the essential question, "How may man make for himself a home in that vastness of strangers and how may he transform that vastness into a home?"

Ibsen, Miller believes, conducted this evaluation, but dramatists after Ibsen have been unable to "bridge the widening gap between the private life and the social life." They usually precipitate one or the other component from the tragic equation: "Our lack of tragedy may be partially accounted for by the turn which modern literature has taken toward the purely psychiatric view of life, or the purely sociological" ("Tragedy and the Common Man"). This fragmented literature reflects contemporary experience: the complexity of society militates against a tragic configuration of its irrationality. "We are so atomized socially that no character in a play can conceivably stand as our vanguard, as our heroic questioner. . . . To think of an individual fulfilling his subjective needs through social action . . . is difficult for us to imagine" ("On Social Plays"). Great drama will not be produced until "a play mixes 'I' with 'we' in a significantly original way. . . . The only materials for a possible new trend in the U.S. are new insights into social and psychological mechanisms; the next original interpretation of these elements, one with the other, will establish a new form."

The task of creating this "new form" has presented Miller—and most notable dramatists of this century—with the severest challenge. How does a writer introduce a social milieu so that its "codes" assume a recognizable and influential presence? How does he show "indignation" as a function of personality—whether the indignation of a rebellious son, a betrayed father, a down-trodden worker, a persecuted citizen, or some combination of these and other identities—rather than as an intellectual abstraction? In short, how does a playwright translate his "way of looking" into a character's way of acting? A character may discuss public issues fluently, but the job of depicting those issues in concrete terms is a formidable one; he may easily exclaim, "I know who I am," but the difficulties involved in giving that self-awareness an emotional content are immense. The solutions Miller proposes in his essays and in his plays supply the index to his achievement as a dramatist. His lifelong effort to integrate the radical "I" with the reactionary "we" has been an impressive one. His shortcomings may well verify his opinion that, given the facts of contemporary life, total success in such an enterprise is inconceivable.

II. THE SEARCH FOR "A NEW FORM"

Miller has never seemed to be particularly intimidated by the problem of finding a dramatic means to interrelate "social and psychological mechanisms." In 1947 he said, "My development is toward an ever-greater examination of human nature. So many people are talking about new form. This to me is an evasion of the problem of playwriting, which is a revelation of human motives regardless of form." A decade later he added [in his *Collected Plays*], "However important considerations of style and form have been to me, they are only means, tools to pry up the well-worn, 'inevitable' surfaces of experience behind which swarm the living thoughts and feelings whose expression is the essential purpose of art." The words "regardless" and "only" belie the tremendous concern Miller has shown for his "tools" throughout his career. If his "examination of human nature" has centered on a single subject, his methods have certainly undergone much modification. In several analyses of his own plays he illuminates those changing artistic strategies and his continuous struggle with the technical questions entailed by his thematic interests.

The most penetrating and comprehensive analysis is his long introduction to the *Collected Plays*. In it he indicates his involvement with three

stylistic modes prevalent in modern drama, which may be labeled the realistic, the expressionistic, and the rhetorical. "I have stood squarely in conventional realism," he declares, and an acknowledgment of a major debt to
Ibsen supports the statement. Although he had gained an appreciation for
the power of "hard facts" from Dostoyevski's *The Brothers Karamazov*, he
learned how "to make the moral world . . . real and evident" by observing
Ibsen's "ability to forge a play upon a factual bedrock. A situation in his
plays is never stated but revealed in terms of hard actions, irrevocable
deeds." More specifically, Ibsen helped Miller answer the "biggest single
[expository] problem, namely, how to dramatize what has gone before":

> If his plays, and his method, do nothing else they reveal the
> evolutionary quality of life. One is constantly aware, in watching
> his plays, of process, change, development. . . . It is therefore
> wrong to imagine that because his first and sometimes his second
> acts devote so much time to a studied revelation of antecedent
> material, his view is static compared to our own. In truth, it is
> profoundly dynamic, for that enormous past was always heavily
> documented to the end that the present be comprehended with
> wholeness, as a moment in a flow of time, and not—as with so
> many modern plays—as a situation without roots.

"What I was after," Miller recalls, "was the wonder in the fact that consequences of actions are as real as the actions themselves."

While he embraced words, gestures, and shapes of the familiar world,
however, he "tried to expand [realism] with an imposition of various forms
in order to speak more directly . . . of what has moved me behind the visible
façades of life." He expanded in two directions. From the start of his career
he wished to enrich the realistic style with an "evaluation of life"—a conscious articulation of ethical judgment. Quite early that wish led to a vexing
predicament: in *The Man Who Had All the Luck*, he realized soon after
completing the work, he had not been able to avoid a rhetorical, or discur-
sive, presentation of his theme. With the next play he determined to "forego"
any sentiments that did not arise naturally from the action. The plan in *All
My Sons* was "to seek cause and effect, hard actions, facts, the geometry of
relationships, and to hold back any tendency to express an idea in itself
unless it was literally forced out of a character's mouth." In this way Miller
thought he would find it possible to elicit a "relatively sharp definition of the
social aspects" without resorting to the discursiveness of the earlier play.

Then he saw that the most significant consequences composing a character's inheritance from past decisions might be emotional, not physical. In

Death of a Salesman, therefore, he introduced an "expressionistic element" to get at the "passion" residing "behind the visible façades." "From the theatrical viewpoint that play . . . broke the bounds, I believe, of a long convention of realism. . . . I had willingly employed expressionism but always to create a subjective truth. . . . I had always been attracted and repelled by the brilliance of German expressionism after World War I, and one aim in *Salesman* was to employ its quite marvelous shorthand for humane, 'felt' characterizations rather than for purposes of demonstration for which the Germans had used it." This "shorthand" reproduced the psychological immediacy of past events: "the *Salesman* image was from the beginning absorbed with the concept that nothing in life comes 'next' but that everything exists together and at the same time within us."

All My Sons represented a compromise between an explicit moralism and a realistic "geometry" of causation; *Death of a Salesman* represented a compromise between rhetorical, realistic, and expressionistic modes. After *Death of a Salesman*, a "preference for plays which seek causation not only in psychology but in society" compelled Miller to curtail his exploration of subjective processes and to return to a more objective frame of reference. In writing *The Crucible* he was still bemused by "a kind of interior mechanism," but he hoped to "lift" his study "out of the morass of subjectivism" with historical data and with evaluative declamation. "It seemed to me then," he writes in a 1960 introduction to *A View from the Bridge*, "that the theater was retreating into an area of psychosexual romanticism, and this at the very moment when great events both at home and abroad cried out for recognition and analytic inspection."

Having "taken a step toward a more self-aware drama" with *The Crucible*, Miller continues in this preface, he decided to advance further into the realm ruled by "codes and ideas of social and ethical importance": the fanaticism of Eddie Carbone can be measured by his willingness to violate "the code of his culture." In another essay, "On Social Plays," Miller states that by the time he wrote *A View from the Bridge* he had abandoned his theory of "interior" causation in favor of "bare" facts and rational commentary. At an earlier stage he probably would have told the story in temporal depth; now he did not want to write "a slowly evolving drama through which the hero's antecedent life forces might, one by one, be brought to light." Without subjective clinical detail interrupting "that clear, clean line of [Eddie's] catastrophe," the "events themselves" could be related swiftly, and the breach of social law would reverberate with "mystery" and "wonderment." In *After the Fall*, again, Miller intended to objectify the "psychological question"—to "present the psychology of men not for its own sake, . . . but primarily as it issues forth in its public importance."

Miller's experimentation with expressionistic, realistic, and rhetorical styles, then, has been conditioned by his overriding desire to declare objective truths about man in society: "our standards of right and wrong, good taste and bad, must in some way come into either conflict or agreement with social standards." A playwright's goal should be to merge "surfaces of experience" (the objective) with "cogent emotional life" (the subjective) and "philosophically or socially meaningful themes" (the analytic) so as to make known the public significance of private engagements. "Drama is akin to the other inventions of man in that it ought to help us to know more, and not merely to spend our feelings. The ultimate justification for a genuine new form is the new and heightened consciousness it creates and makes possible—a consciousness of causation in the light of known but hitherto inexplicable effects." Miller's aim as a craftsman has been to "make real on stage as in life that part of man which, through passion, seeks awareness. There is no contradiction between the two."

III. THE PROBLEM OF PERSPECTIVE

Arthur Miller and Eugene O'Neill have done more than other American dramatists to "relate the subjective to the objective truth": *Death of a Salesman* and O'Neill's *Long Day's Journey into Night* are two of the finest works in the American theater. Contrary to Miller's assertion, however, there *is* in his plays a contradiction between passion and awareness, between irrational impulse and rational concept. His best dialogue mirrors psychological conditions, yet he constantly returns to the formal generalization; he can skillfully manipulate emotional tension, yet he seeks aesthetic detachment; his figures act most intelligibly in a family context, yet he feels obliged to make explicit their connection with a social "environment." Miller sees his principal subject—the drive for self-justification—primarily as an *internal* process activated by "mechanisms" that repress or involuntarily recall shameful memories and motives, that effect rapid transitions between taut and relaxed moods. When his characters fervently defend egocentric attitudes, their futility evokes a genuine sense of terror and pathos that indirectly but powerfully reinforces his thesis on the necessity for "meaningful" accommodation in society. When, on the other hand, his characters intelligently reform, their self-knowledge remains only a rhetorical promise. After their fall and recovery the mature new-men—Lawrence Newman, David Frieber, Chris Keller, Biff Loman, John Proctor, Gay

Langland, Quentin, Leduc, Von Berg, and the Franz brothers—predicate rather than model their liberating insights. A tendency to impose judgment upon action—the tendency Miller worried about after writing his first Broadway play, *The Man Who Had All the Luck*—has prevented him from achieving the harmony of styles he has long sought. His attempt to enlarge the "interior psychological question" with "codes and ideas of social and ethical importance" has distorted his subjective perspective and so compromised his exceptional talent.

A review of his symbolic, structural, and verbal techniques substantiates this conclusion. Miller has been relatively fortunate in finding apt metaphors to signify the implications of a "gap between the private life and the social life." Most of his symbolic images, it is true, are drawn along simple lines—a carousel that conceals hatred (*Focus*); a fruitful tree destroyed in its prime (*All My Sons*); "green leaves" blotted out by the hard outlines of apartment buildings, a flute song displaced by childish nonsense from a wire recorder, a wife's praise erased by a whore's laugh (*Death of a Salesman*); a dingy warehouse harboring hopeless inmates (*A Memory of Two Mondays*); a herd of mustangs moving toward extinction (*The Misfits*); a ruined tower that memorializes horrors committed by "ordinary" men (*After the Fall*); feathers and a broken pot guarded as if they were life itself (*Incident at Vichy*); a "massive," discarded armchair (*The Price*).

Just as obviously, many of Miller's workers—a fearful personnel manager in an anti-Semitic corporation (*Focus*) and an unscrupulous industrialist (*All My Sons*), a frustrated salesman (*Death of a Salesman*) and a dispirited policeman (*The Price*), dehumanized laborers (*A Memory of Two Mondays*) and displaced cowboys (*The Misfits*)—find little spiritual "sustenance" in their trades. Men who look for a satisfying social role in a productive occupation—Chris Keller, Biff Loman, Kenneth and Bert, Gay Langland, Quentin, and Walter Franz—are disappointed; even the reborn Lawrence Newman faces a future as a "glorified usher to salesmen." In *Incident at Vichy*, one of only two plays set in a foreign locale, the situation is worse: none of the prisoners—from Leduc, a psychiatrist, to Von Berg, an aristocratic non-worker, to the Gypsy, who does odd (or illegal) jobs—can possibly make positive use of his abilities in his country. Despite his acquaintance with a wide variety of trades as a youth, Miller never envisioned a profession—except, perhaps, his own—that could unite its practitioner with his society in mutually beneficial labor.

Taken symbolically, these vocations and images could be said to indicate the misuse of natural talent brought about by an incongruity between personal and social objectives in contemporary urban culture. As such, they are rather facile indications. A subtler, more extended occupational metaphor that objectively represents the individual's malaise in society is the pursuit of justice through law. In Miller's plays, with their rhythm of accusation and defense, the defendant invariably fails to obtain equity and must resort to extralegal means to protect his rights.

Lawrence Newman forges a new code of conduct after he perceives the inadequacy of the mores to which he had subscribed and the inability of the law to relieve racial discrimination. In *All My Sons*, a courtroom drama in essence if not in setting, the trial metaphor assumes greater importance. Joe Keller commits fraud and involuntary homicide, conspires to incriminate his partner, and evades detection until his son (with the help of George, a lawyer) prosecutes, finds him guilty, rejects his appeal, and delivers what amounts to a death sentence. Both Chris and his father call upon principles beyond the jurisdiction of formal law; each defends his principle with a fierceness that makes the legal question seem petty in comparison. In *Death of a Salesman*, again a minor character, Bernard, chooses law as his profession, and again a father stands accused, then condemned by his son for a breach of trust far more serious than, though associated with, his technical transgression (adultery).

Eddie Carbone brings on disaster by upholding a statute (against illegal immigration), not by violating one, but—as with Joe Keller, Willy Loman, and Eddie's accuser, Marco—his justification transcends the realm of jurisprudence. Institutional procedures are powerless to secure for him his paternal "rights" or to prevent Rodolpho from "stealing" his niece. "The law is not interested in this," his impassive attorney tells him; "you have no recourse in the law." Victor Franz, retiring from police work, sees his career as "a little unreal," and in *The Creation of the World* man comes out guilty even when God argues for him. Miller's central metaphorical statement of the law's insufficiency occurs in *After the Fall*, whose protagonist rejects the legal profession after having adopted its mode of operation in his personal life. Quentin learns (as does Eddie Carbone) that the great limitation of the legal mode is an incapacity to account for, much less to deal with, emotional needs. Although his original outlook persists—he continues to discuss human behavior in terms of moralistic formulas ("this pointless litigation of existence before an empty bench")—he gives up his practice in the hope of arriving at more humane knowledge.

In these works the legal system for redress of grievance is seen to be almost irrelevant to the protagonist's defense of a "conception, however misguided, of right, dignity, and justice." In *Incident at Vichy*, in *The Crucible*, and in Miller's adaptation of Ibsen's *An Enemy of the People*, the system of public morality becomes, through agents acting in its name, the active perpetrator of injustice. The trial of integrity is consequently tied more closely to a courtroom or jail terminology. *Incident at Vichy* deals with the supreme perverters of law in recent times. As in Kafka's *The Trial*, the rationale that justifies political murder ("there are no persons any-more") appears bizarre and irrational to those victimized by it. Only Von Berg penetrates the ethical obscurity by reasserting, in an act of self-sacrifice, the responsibility of individual conscience. Similarly, John Proctor gives up his life to confirm a principle of enlightened self-determination intolerable to the Salem judges. (Before the hearing and the ordeal in jail, Proctor suffered a private trial at home: "I come into a court when I come into this house!" he complained to his wife, who would not forgive his liaison with Abigail.)

In his adaptation of Ibsen's *An Enemy of the People* (1950), Miller reiterated with an abundance of legalistic set-speeches his belief that public antipathy can provide a grueling test for a nonconformist who dares question social standards. As in *Focus, The Crucible*, and *Incident at Vichy*, a community's insanity arouses indignation in a "lonely" battler. The issue is almost allegorical in its polarization of good and evil: Honesty, personified by brave Dr. Stockmann, debates (again in a trial setting) with Evil, personified by smug middle-class materialists—the "people." During the debate Stockmann exposes the bourgeois immorality, self-interest, and blindness that had masqueraded as communal justice, enterprise, and wisdom. "The majority," he declares, "is never right until it *does* right." The fact that Stockmann, in common with most of Miller's chief figures, is forced to look beyond juridical criteria for a tenable standard of justice calls into question the social order founded upon those criteria. "There doesn't seem to be much of a law," a character laments in *All My Sons*; "all the law is not in a book," Marco states in *A View from the Bridge*. Where law is superfluous or malign, the trial process becomes an ironic metaphor for the pursuit of self-respect.

Miller incorporated the accusation-defense rhythm of a trial into almost all his major plays. Despite his wide-ranging experiments with form, the narrative schemes of *All My Sons, Death of a Salesman, The Crucible, A View from the Bridge*, and *After the Fall* are remarkably alike. In each work hidden guilt is first referred to covertly, then bared in a climactic revelation—a scheme based upon Ibsen's exhibitions of the inescapable causal movement from past action to present reaction. The secrets and the methods with which they are brought to light vary. Eddie Carbone obstinately suppresses *two* secrets—betrayal of the immigrants (an objective fact) and ardor for his niece (a "cast of mind"). Joe Keller and Willy Loman also conceal both their crimes and their moral frailty; John Proctor *confesses* his sins; Quentin concludes that *all* men are guilty. In *All My Sons*, in *The Crucible*, and in *A View from the Bridge*, the sin is suggested by verbal allusions and by the protagonist's behavior; *Death of a Salesman* and *After the Fall* modify that procedure with memory-surveys. Since the protagonist fears discovery—he usually hesitates to admit his offenses even to himself—gradual exposition generates suspense by exploiting the discrepancy between inward reality and outward appearance. "Who can ever know what will be discovered?" Alfieri muses.

Revelation ensures a surprising transition from one issue to another. As the secret comes into view, an antagonism developed at the beginning of each play gives way to a more urgent opposition. Thus attention is transferred from an argument between Chris and Kate to an argument between Chris and Joe (*All My Sons*); from a present to a past father-son dilemma (*Death of a Salesman*); from a struggle between the Proctors and Abigail to one between John Proctor and the judges who have condemned him (*The Crucible*); from the Eddie-Rodolpho to the Eddie-Marco duel (*A View from the Bridge*); and from Quentin's dialogue with Louise to that with Maggie (*After the Fall*). Both before and after the transfer, dramatic interest centers on only one of the combatants: Keller's fear replaces his wife's as the crucial subject; Willy's failures in the past, his failures in the present; Proctor's final decision, Abigail's machinations; Eddie's response to Marco, the response to Rodolpho; Quentin's self-justification in the second marriage, that in the first.

This complex format has an outstanding weakness: the resolution of the second issue tends to occur after the emotional climax, an outcome that is likely to reduce the impact and coherence of the primary progression of character in the preceding action. Chris Keller's first engagement with his father was emotionally climactic but ethically inconclusive. The subsequent rematch forfeits excitement generated by the gradual development of Joe Keller's anxiety; during the last act Chris diverts attention from the protagonist's standpoint with speeches on social responsibility. Although the focus of interest belatedly shifts from the harried father to the outraged son, however, the decisive conflict is at least confined to a single set of opponents. In *The Crucible*, contrarily, the public problem of witchcraft (which supersedes the private problem of love-jealousy) splits into two relatively separate power struggles: one involves Abigail, Proctor, and the girls during the hearing; the other, Proctor and his jailors after it. These struggles, loosely joined by Miller's implied theory that society can be saved by its morally mature citizens, come to *independent crises* ending respectively in mass hysteria (the melodramatic highpoint) and personal honesty (Proctor's refusal to confess to witchcraft). Until the fourth act, the social implications of the play arise directly from psychological origins; then the causal connection is abruptly severed. A *View from the Bridge* displays another anticlimactic resolution. The emergence of a second antagonist moves the battle for respect from a family to a community arena, but it blurs "that clear, clean line" of the original (and critical) confrontation, a result compounded by the narrator's propensity for myth-making.

Eager to advance his concept of social "relatedness," Miller fails to honor in these plays the structural rule he observed in Ibsen, Beethoven, and Dostoyevsky: "above all, the precise collision of inner themes during, not before or after, the high dramatic scenes. . . . The holding back of climax until it was ready, the grasp of the rising line and the unwillingness to divert to an easy climax until the true one was ready." He avoids anticlimax in *After the Fall* by unfolding Quentin's problem and solution concurrently, allowing only a summary statement of the solution at the ending. Unfortunately, the skeletal, poorly integrated memory sequences inhibit the movement toward significant climax. The double-issue design is wholly successful only in *Death of a Salesman* because there the articulation of value does not become narratively (or verbally) intrusive. Like Chris Keller, Biff Loman goes home again to clarify his "revolutionary questioning," and others also offer interpretive comments. But this activity, far from redirecting attention from one character or issue to another after the play's tensional peak, merely expedites the outcome already predicted by the Salesman's spiritual collapse and makes possible a measured transition from the chaos of the climax to the numbed calm of the denouement. Willy Loman consistently channels the flow of tension; his "fanaticism" unifies psychological and sociological sources of tragedy.

Miller's construction, if rarely flawless, is never formless. His metaphors, if sometimes obvious, are sometimes subtle. It is the dialogue that swings between extremes of brilliance and insipidity. Colloquial speech may be heard in an amazing variety of accents—Irish, Swedish, German, Sicilian, Slavic, Barbados, Yiddish, Puritan, Brooklyn, Southwestern, and Midwestern. *After the Fall* and *Incident at Vichy*, in fact, were the first works that did not make extensive use of subliterate English (except for Maggie's New York locutions and childish inanities, which convey a certain charm and a certain mental barrenness). Whether in historical, regional, or foreign dialect, Miller's dialogue is most telling when it works by implication, not by explication.

Explicit analyses of motivation may, of course, serve a legitimate and even commendable purpose by establishing a rational perspective. Thus Biff Loman and Charley reflect on the meaning of Willy's existence; the misfits as philosophers explain the misfits as doers; Quentin during his psychoanalysis contemplates Quentin before; Leduc and Von Berg answer the question puzzling the other prisoners; the debates in *The Price* and *The Creation of the World* propose policies to secure deliverance from guilt. Rhetorical differences corresponding to differences in perceptiveness are often pronounced: the abstruseness of Shory, Hester, and David Frieber contrasts with the folksiness of their friends in *The Man Who Had All the Luck*; the incisiveness of Newman's thoughts contrasts with the triteness of his conversation; Chris Keller's abstractness, with his father's solidity; Proctor's eloquence, with the girls' incoherence; Alfieri's fluency, with Eddie's awkwardness; the lyricism of *A Memory of Two Mondays* with the slanginess; Gay's pretentiousness, with Roslyn's naiveté; Walter's formality, with Solomon's simplicity. Too often in these instances, however, "analytic inspection" receives disproportionate emphasis, produces artificial wisdom, and unbalances the interplay between idiomatically authentic, emotionally intense, and ethically rational language styles.

At other times, trivial homespun talk, unable to bridge the "gap" separating passion from formal communication, dumbly masks unspeakable humiliation, wrath, or sorrow. Then Miller's writing attains its greatest power. Joe Keller's bluff words resound with increasing apprehension: "because it's good money, there's nothing wrong with that money. . . . What have I got to hide? What the hell is the matter with you?" Interrogating his son with driving insistence, Keller harshly answers each question he raises:

> Jail? You want me to go to jail? If you want me to go, say so! . . . I'll tell you why you can't say it. Because you know I don't belong there. Because you know! . . . Who worked for nothin' in that war? When they work for nothin', I'll work for nothin'. Did they ship a gun or a truck outa Detroit before they got their price? Is that clean? It's dollars and cents, nickels and dimes; war and peace, it's nickels and dimes, what's clean? Half the Goddam country is gotta go if I go! That's why you can't tell me.

The conviction ringing in these rhetorical questions derives less from a businessman's self-righteousness than from a father's desperation.

In a similar way Willy Loman's commonplace locutions define uncommon motives. "He won't starve. None a them starve," Charley advises concerning Biff, "forget about him." Willy answers with the poignantly simple sentence, "then what have I got to remember?" Longer passages touch upon, rather than belabor, specific ideas exposed by the action. In her concluding remark Linda alludes quite laconically to her financial insecurity, to her efforts to keep the "home" intact, and above all to her inability to comprehend her husband's strange compulsion: "Why did you do it? I search and search and I search, and I can't understand it, Willy. I made the last payment on the house today. Today, dear. And there'll be nobody home. . . . We're free and clear. We're free."

The Crucible, like *Death of a Salesman* (and all of Miller's plays), contains some self-conscious oratory. In neither work does this detract from the dynamics of character, theme, and tension (perhaps the long historical footnotes in *The Crucible* helped assuage Miller's speculative bent). The Puritan dialect may sound archaic and formal to a present-day audience, but it can be as impressive in its monosyllabic directness as contemporary English. "It were a fearsome man," Rebecca eulogizes over one of the witch-hunt victims. "Spite only keeps me silent," Proctor says; "it is hard to give the lie to dogs." A few fanciful metaphors relieve the verbal plainness ("I see now your spirit twists around the single error of my life, and I will never tear it free!"), and Tituba's exotic, faintly humorous Barbados inflection contributes additional color.

Like Tituba, Joe Keller, and Willy Loman, Eddie Carbone in *A View from the Bridge* expresses fearfulness through a comfortably ungrammatical, sometimes comic idiom. "Listen," he warns Catherine, "I could tell you things about Louis which you wouldn't wave to him no more." His contorted syntax registers sharper pain as, ashamed and embarrassed, he tries to dissuade his niece from marriage. In one passage his words wander about in a sobbing rhythm before stumbling to their apologetic petition:

> I was just tellin' Beatrice . . . if you wanna go out, like . . . I mean I realize maybe I kept you home too much. Because he's the first guy you ever knew, y'know? I mean now that you got a job, you might meet some fellas, and you get a different idea, y'know? I mean you could always come back to him, you're still only kids, the both of yiz. What's the hurry? Maybe you'll get around a little bit, you grow up a little more, maybe you'll see different in a couple of months. I mean you be surprised, it don't have to be him. [Miller's ellipses]

When suppressed feeling threatens to burst the everyday verbal "façade" in lines such as these, the common man's language becomes emotionally resonant. That resonance marks the distinctive quality of Arthur Miller's achievement.

NEIL CARSON

A View from the Bridge
and the Expansion of Vision

In spite of the growing popularity of his plays both in America and abroad in the early 1950s, Miller came increasingly to feel that he was being misunderstood. *Death of a Salesman,* which he had written half in "laughter and joy," had been received as a work of the direst pessimism. When in his next play, Miller deliberately set out to create a more articulate hero, he had little more success in communicating his ideas. Not one reviewer of the original production of *The Crucible* mentioned what to Miller was the central theme of the work—the handing over of conscience to another. The sense of bewilderment and frustration resulting from this apparent incomprehension on the part of audiences and critics alike led Miller to make more explicit public statements about his aims as a playwright. In a series of essays, speeches and introductions to his plays published between 1949 and 1960, Miller expounded a comprehensive theory of drama which constitutes one of the most complete statements on the subject by a contemporary playwright. It would be pleasant if one could report that these essays have effectively dispelled all misunderstanding concerning Miller's work. Unfortunately that is far from the case. Indeed in some respects Miller's dramatic criticism serves only to complicate issues by emphasising the differences between what the playwright apparently intends to say and what in fact he does communicate. Few of his published statements are more confusing than the several explanations he has given for the writing and revision of *A View from the Bridge.*

In reflecting on the hostile criticism of *The Crucible* (much of which

From *Arthur Miller.* © 1982 by Neil Carson. Grove Press, Inc., 1982.

described the play as cold) Miller came to the conclusion that the implication that the play would have been improved by a greater emphasis on the subjective lives of the characters was wrong. What was needed, on the contrary, was not more subjectivism, but more self-awareness. The failure of modern realism to reveal more than the surface of life, Miller came to believe, was a result of the inability of playwrights and audiences to agree upon "the pantheon of forces and values" which must lie behind that surface. In his next play, Miller resolved, he would transcend realism and create a form in which it would be possible to join feeling to awareness. Although he did not know what form such a drama would take, he felt that one model of the kind of wholeness he admired in drama was tragedy.

Tragedy can be described as an attempt to make some positive statement about human life in the face of defeat and death. It emerged in ancient Greece, and had a second flowering in the Renaissance, both periods of expansion and questioning after relatively more settled periods of faith. Tragedy addresses the problem of apparently undeserved suffering, and attempts to vindicate the claims of religion in the face of seeming injustice. The Greek answer (reflecting the Greek attitude to the gods) proclaims the power of fate and the weakness and blindness of man. In the tragic meeting between man and circumstance, man's error is acknowledged, but the emphasis is on external fate. In Aristotle's phrase, tragedy inspires in the spectator a mingling of "pity" for the protagonist and "terror" of the power and mystery of the gods.

Christian tragedies, such as those of Shakespeare, put greater emphasis on the human flaw. The suffering in Christian tragedy (often including the destruction of innocent bystanders such as Ophelia or Desdemona) is not the consequence of divine fiat, but of human passion or evil. As in Greek tragedy, the protagonist in Shakespeare must be removed before a healthy order can be restored. But because of the different emphasis, the catharsis in Christian tragedy is different. Pity for the protagonist is mixed with another emotion directed towards the heavens which is not so much terror as a kind of reverent dread. The sufferings of a Hamlet or a Lear are tolerable because they take place in a universe which is essentially understandable and moral.

The problem for the twentieth-century dramatist who would deal seriously with the most profound questions of life and death is that the background of reassurance once provided by religious faith no longer exists. In the face of almost universal scepticism few contemporary writers any longer attempt to present suffering as meaningful. Modern drama has tended on the whole to document man's frustration, defeat or despair, and to find its only significance in subjective experience. In a series of essays written after

1949, Miller attempted to formulate a theory of tragedy which would re-introduce the concept of "victory" into drama.

His earliest pronouncements on the nature of tragedy appeared in the New York newspapers. For Miller, the basic ingredients in tragedy are the protagonist's sense of indignation, and his compulsion to "evaluate himself justly." All the tragic heroes from Orestes to Macbeth, we are told, are destroyed in attempting to obtain their rightful place in society. What distinguishes the tragic hero from the mass of ordinary men is his willingness to question and attack the scheme of things that degrades him. This challenge of the seemingly stable cosmos produces terror in an audience which is fearful of being torn away from their image of what and who they are in the world. But it also enlightens. The spectacle of the hero's attack suggests an evil in his environment; his destruction hints at the existence of a moral law. The conflict in tragedy, therefore, is not between man and some irresistible fate; it shows the hero struggling against social forces that can be changed or overcome. For, as Miller says, tragedy must always show how the catastrophe might have been avoided, how good might have been allowed to express itself instead of succumbing to evil.

Miller's tragic aesthetic differs in many significant respects from traditional classical and Christian theories. In part, these differences can be traced to more recent ideas. For example, it owes a great deal to the romantic celebration of heroes such as Satan, Prometheus and Faust. It owes something, too, to "Ibsenism" as defined by George Bernard Shaw, and not a little to the social drama of the 1930s. But it is also a product of Miller's own exploration of dramatic form. In his plays from *The Man Who Had All the Luck* to *Death of a Salesman* Miller had been concerned with balancing defeat and victory. In *All My Sons* the narrow, family-centred morality of Joe Keller is replaced at the end of the play by the higher consciousness of Chris. In *Death of a Salesman,* Willy's belief in material success is transcended by Biff's self-fulfilment.

In planning the form of *A View from the Bridge,* Miller seems to have been determined that the "generalized significance" of the play would be made plain to all. To ensure that his meaning could not be mistaken, he introduced a chorus figure who could address the audience directly. Characteristically *A View from the Bridge* is a two-level play in which the psychological and social elements seem sometimes at odds. Eddie Carbone, a longshoreman in the Red Hook district of Brooklyn, and his wife Beatrice have been responsible for the upbringing of their niece Catherine since the death of her parents when she was very young. Catherine is now seventeen, and Eddie's affection for her as a daughter has developed into something much more powerful without either Eddie or Catherine being aware of the change. Some hint of the possessive and unnatural form of his love is given by his reluctance to let Catherine wear high heels, but the full power of his passion does not emerge until Catherine wants to leave home to get married. At that point Eddie's jealousy brings him into direct and tragic conflict with his niece's boyfriend.

The social level of the play deals with the strict code of loyalty of the Sicilian-American community in which Eddie lives and with the tragic consequences of Eddie's infraction of that code. The crisis is precipitated by the arrival of Rodolpho and Marco, Beatrice's Italian relatives, who have been smuggled into the United States illegally. The Carbones take their relatives into their home where they provide them with food and shelter, but tensions between the visitors and their host build up quickly when it becomes apparent that Rodolpho and Catherine are beginning to fall in love. The antagonism reaches a climax when Eddie returns home early one day to find Rodolpho and Catherine in the bedroom. Eddie orders Rodolpho to leave whereupon Catherine starts to go with him. Eddie grasps her arm and says,

> You goin' with him. You goin' with him, heh? (*He grabs her face in the vise of his two hands.*) You goin' with him! (*He kisses her on the mouth as she pulls at his arms: he will not let go, keeps his face pressed against hers.*)

Unable to admit the true nature of his feeling for Catherine, Eddie converts his jealousy of Rodolpho into a conviction that he is a homosexual and only interested in Catherine as a means of obtaining American citizenship. He appeals to Alfieri, the lawyer in the district, for a legal means of stopping what he has come to consider Rodolpho's theft of Catherine. Alfieri, sensing the true cause of Eddie's torment but unable to make him see it, tries to tell him that "somebody had to come for her . . . sooner or later." He also warns Eddie against betraying Rodolpho to the immigration authorities, reminding him of the strict code against informers in the community.

> You won't have a friend in the world, Eddie! Even those who understand will turn against you.

Ignoring Alfieri's warning, Eddie phones the immigration officials who come and arrest Marco and Rodolpho as well as two other recently arrived immigrants. As he is led away, Marco spits in Eddie's face, and in front of his neighbours accuses him of betraying them.

The final scene shows Marco returning for vengeance. We are told that he has prayed in the church, but since he carries no weapon it is unclear whether he intends to kill Eddie or simply punish him with a beating. Waiting for Marco, Eddie refuses to run and tries once more to separate Rodolpho and Catherine. Beatrice begs him to release Catherine, saying of Rodolpho, "It's her husband! Let her go." When Catherine and Rodolpho start to leave,

> (*Eddie lunges and catches her: he holds her, and she weeps up into his face. And he kisses her on the lips.*)
> EDDIE (*like a lover, out of his madness*): It's me, ain't it?

When Marco finally arrives, Eddie accuses them of stealing Catherine from him and of making his name "like a dirty rag." "I want my good name, Marco! You took my name!" Eddie pulls a knife, but Marco turns it on him, and he is fatally wounded. As he falls forward, he

> (*crawls a yard to Catherine. She raises her face away—but she does not move as he reaches over and grasps her leg, and looking up at her, he seems puzzled, questioning, betrayed.*)
> EDDIE: Catherine—why?

The play ends with a speech by Alfieri which presumably sums up Miller's understanding of the "generalized significance" of the story as he has come to see it.

> Most of the time we settle for half,
> And I like it better.
> And yet, when the tide is right
> And the green smell of the sea
> Floats in through my window,
> The waves of this bay
> Are the waves against Siracusa.
> And I see a face that suddenly seems carved;
> The eyes look like tunnels
> Leading back toward some ancestral beach
> Where all of us once lived.
> And I wonder at those times
> How much of all of us
> Really lives there yet,
> And when we will truly have moved on,
> On and away from that dark place,
> That world that has fallen to stones?

This version of the play seems to be a kind of Euripidean tragedy of passion in which the protagonist is overcome by an irresistible and self-destructive madness. The implication of the final speech is that such passion is essentially primitive, an aspect of human nature that belongs to a dead past, and that it is time that men moved on towards a more rational form of behaviour and society. But this implication is by no means clear and, within the context of the action of the play alone, Eddie seems to exhibit a few of the qualities of the tragic protagonist as Miller had defined them in his essays.

This is all the more surprising since Miller had obviously been giving considerable thought to the nature of Greek drama during the writing of *A View from the Bridge*. His ideas are summed up in an essay entitled "On Social Plays" which appeared as an introduction to the published version of the play a couple of months after the Broadway opening. Here he describes the wholeness of Greek drama which he feels has been lost on the modern stage, and discusses a new form of social drama which he feels might recapture the Greek breadth of vision.

The principal way in which classical drama differs from modern plays, Miller feels, is in its concern with ultimate law. The Greek dramatist was interested in psychology, but only as a means to a larger end which was the discovery of the Grand Design, the right way to live together. The grandeur of Greek drama was its ability to treat both the private life *and* the social context. "For when the Greek thought of the right way to live it was a whole concept, it meant a way to live that would create citizens who were brave in war, had a sense of responsibility to the polis [city state] in peace, and were also developed as individual personalities."

Modern drama, Miller thinks, has lost the ability to deal with the whole man. The "social drama" from Ibsen and Shaw to the left-wing playwrights of the 1930s has put too much emphasis on social causation. On the other hand, the "psychological drama" is often nothing more than a purely private examination of individuality for the sake of the examination or for art's sake. What is needed is a new social drama which will combine the approach of the Greek theatre with modern discoveries in psychology and economics.

In this essay Miller is clearly addressing problems related to the writing of a modern tragedy such as *A View from the Bridge*. The dilemma facing the modern dramatist is twofold says Miller: first, we no longer believe that some ultimate sense can be made of social causation, and second, no single individual can any longer be considered representative of a whole people. How then does the contemporary playwright portray the kind of tragic figure who would have the power to pass over the boundary of the known social law in order to discover a way of life which would yield excellence? Miller's solution in the first version of *A View from the Bridge* was to create an objective narrator who could see and describe the larger context which was hidden from the hero, and to write about a relatively closed society in which the conflict between the protagonist and the social law would engage the passions of the whole community.

There is some evidence that even before the production of the play, Miller may have been dissatisfied with the solutions he attempted in it. A central problem was his inability to grasp what he felt to be the ultimate meaning of the story. When he first heard the tale from a waterfront worker in Brooklyn, he felt that the weaving together of the lives of the characters seemed almost the work of fate. But in dramatising it he had been unable to define the objective and subjective elements that made that fate. Consequently he felt that a certain mystery remained that he could not account for.

During the rehearsals for the production, Miller and the director, Martin Ritt, strove to achieve a non-naturalistic style of acting and design which would encourage a more objective response, so that the audience's emotional identification with Eddie would not overwhelm their ability to judge his actions in the social context. To this end, excessive and arbitrary gestures were eliminated, the set was designed to be suggestive of the classical parallels Miller saw in the story. The problem was that neither the director (a former member of the Group Theatre) nor the actors had any experience with this kind of staging. The result was not a success.

Brooks Atkinson of the *New York Times* probably reflected the general reaction when he criticised the very effects Miller and Ritt had used to distance the audience. "Mr. Miller's principle of underwriting," he wrote, "may have been ill-advised. . . . Eddie's deficiency as a tragic hero is simply that Miller has not told us enough about him." Atkinson went on to say that far from being a "hero" Eddie seemed mean and vicious, and got just about what he deserved. The characters of the wife and niece were also criticised for being too sketchy. The actors seemed to portray abstract ideas rather than human beings, and the performance reminded Atkinson of the style of the Group Theatre "all mind and nerves" and no flesh.

A second circumstance that made Miller dissatisfied with the first version of the play was his discovery of his own personal connection with it. After seeing the production several times, he suddenly realised that the piece was in some part an analogy to situations in his own life. What those situations were Miller never explained. Perhaps he saw in Eddie's infatuation for Catherine a parallel to his own interest in Marilyn Monroe. Possibly he came to think that his total condemnation of Eddie the informer was simplistic in view of the inroads passion had made in his own life? Whatever the nature of the new insights Miller had into the story, when the opportunity arose to have the play produced in London, he felt he had to rewrite it to include them.

In the revised play, the characters of Beatrice and Catherine were considerably enlarged, and they played a more direct role in Eddie's fate. Furthermore the London production was conceived in a much more realistic mode. The set was a highly detailed reconstruction of the Brooklyn apartment with its surroundings of alleys and fire-escapes, and most of the poetry of the first version was eliminated or the ideas expressed in the vivid Brooklyn argot of the neighbourhood. The classically trained British actors were better able than their American counterparts to find an acting style that would move easily from the highly emotional to the sedately dignified.

Even more interesting than the alterations in form, however, are the changes Miller made in the central character. In this revised version, Miller plays down Eddie's physical passion for Catherine and focuses instead on his relationship to Marco. In the concluding minutes of the play it is Marco's insult, not Rodolpho's rivalry, which is foremost in Eddie's mind. When Beatrice attempts to make him confront his real motive, Eddie turns away from the truth.

> BEATRICE: Who could give you your name? . . . if [Marco] goes on his knees, what is he got to give you? That's not what you want.
>
> EDDIE: Don't bother me!
>
> BEATRICE: You want something else, Eddie, and you can never have her! . . . The truth is not as bad as blood, Eddie! I'm tellin' you the truth—tell her good-by forever.

Confronted with this truth, however, Eddie cannot accept it and cries out his repudiation, "That's what you think of me—that I could have such a thought?" When he goes out to challenge Marco shouting, "I want my name," therefore, he is persisting in a deluded course of action. Eddie's concern with his "name," though superficially similar to John Proctor's at the end of *The Crucible,* is in reality very different. Whereas Proctor comes to see that his name is something only he can evaluate justly, Eddie believes falsely that his name is in the custody of his accusers. In the revised version, Eddie dies in the arms of Beatrice, and Miller probably intends to suggest by this that he finally comes to some kind of acceptance of his nature and his strange love.

Alfieri's final speech in the two-act version is very different from the original. Paradoxically the emphasis seems to shift away from the universal and primitive nature of Eddie's passion to the unique qualities of the man.

> Most of the time now we settle for half and I like it better. But the truth is holy, and even as I know how wrong he was, and his death useless, I tremble, for I confess that something perversely pure calls to me from his memory—not purely good, but himself purely, for he allowed himself to be wholly known and for that I will love him more than all my sensible clients. And yet, it is better to settle for half, it must be! And so I mourn him—I admit it—with a certain . . . alarm.

The relationship of all this to the play and to Eddie's character seems to me to be extremely obscure. Alfieri is contrasting the sensible people who settle for half and the potentially tragic individuals who cannot let well enough alone. According to Miller's theory of tragedy, such individuals are driven to act when others would retire, and in so acting they cause the scheme of things to act with retributive violence against them. But in what way can Eddie's actions be interpreted as a challenge of the "stable cosmos" and how do they lead to the discovery of new understanding or a moral law? What "holy truth" has been pursued by this protagonist or revealed by his death?

Superficially it would seem that the evil in this play is not in the environment, but in Eddie, and in this respect the play is fairly traditional. In the revised version of the play, however, Miller has introduced lines to suggest that he is contrasting the Sicilian-American code of revenge with Beatrice's plea for forgiveness, and that he intends to imply that the tragedy would not have happened if Eddie had acknowledged the dark side of his nature. But these themes (if indeed they are implicit) are overshadowed by the spectacle of Eddie's slide into madness. The strangely inappropriate nature of Alfieri's concluding comment suggests that Miller has still not fathomed the mystery at the centre of this story, and that its meaning still eludes him.

An opportunity to try for a third time to come to grips with the story of Eddie Carbone arose during the rehearsals for the Paris production. The director, Peter Brook, was apparently informed that no French audience would accept the notion that Eddie and Catherine could be unaware of the nature of the love between them. For this production, therefore, Miller wrote a third ending in which Marco refuses to kill Eddie. Isolated by his neighbours who make him realise that he himself is responsible for the loss of his good name, Eddie kills himself. This ending seems in many ways the most intellectually satisfying, although it is perhaps psychologically improbable.

When he was preparing his plays for the collected edition of his dramatic works, it was the London version of *A View from the Bridge* that he selected to be printed. In the introduction to his *Collected Plays,* Miller returned again to a consideration of the play and what he had learned from the two very different productions. His original conception of the character of Eddie had been, he felt, too objective. In revising the play he found it possible to identify much more fully with Eddie and to make him more sympathetic to the audience. This made it more possible to mourn a man who, although guilty of the most serious offences, nevertheless had a certain dignity. Even more important than the insight into Eddie's character, however, were the lessons Miller learned about dramatic form. By comparing the reception of the play in London and New York he became convinced that the ultimate test of a play's effectiveness was performance in the theatre. "A play," he wrote, "ought to make sense to common-sense people. . . . It is their innate conservatism which, I think, is and ought to be the barrier to excess in experiment and the exploitation of the bizarre." Miller's choice of the second version of *A View from the Bridge* for inclusion in his *Collected Plays* suggests a repudiation of the "distancing" effects he had experimented with at first. He became convinced that "the theater is above all else an instrument of passion." To create new forms, requires greater attention, not less, to the "inexorable, common, pervasive conditions of existence."

C. W. E. BIGSBY

Drama from a Living Center

A*ll My Sons* is ostensibly a play about morality. Joe Keller, a war-time manufacturer of aircraft engines, had been charged with supplying defective equipment which led to the death of twenty-one pilots. At the trial, however, he had denied responsibility, allowing his timid partner to take the blame. Having been exonerated, he has successfully reestablished his business and though his neighbours still believe him to be guilty they have apparently accepted him back into their social life. But relief at his acquittal is tempered by grief at the loss of his son, himself a pilot, reported missing, presumed dead.

At the time of the play, some three years later, that son's fiancée, Ann (daughter of Joe Keller's business partner), arrives to become engaged to the dead boy's brother, Chris Keller. This provokes a crisis for his mother, since she has refused to accept the fact of her son's death and has seen Ann's failure to marry as evidence of her similar faith in his survival. The planned marriage, therefore, involves laying the ghost of the dead son. But, more significantly, acceptance of her son's death also forces her to acknowledge a connection between that event and what she knows to be her husband's guilt. The situation is compounded when Ann's brother George arrives to confront Joe with that guilt. And though he fails to wring a confession from Joe the imminent marriage does. For Chris's mother plays her final card in order to prevent the marriage which will signal the end of her hope. She reveals her husband's guilt to her son. But she and her husband are finally

From *A Critical Introduction to Twentieth-Century American Drama 2: Tennessee Williams, Arthur Miller, Edward Albee.* © 1984 by C. W. E. Bigsby. Cambridge University Press, 1984.

defeated by a letter which Ann now reveals, a letter in which the missing son had announced his intention of committing suicide because of his father's actions. Stunned into accepting responsibility for his actions, Joe Keller shoots himself, bequeathing a kind of freedom to his son, who will accept no other inheritance.

On the surface the play is an extension of earlier themes. It is an assertion of the need for the individual to accept full responsibility for his actions, to acknowledge the reality of a world in which the idea of brotherhood is an active principle rather than a simple piety. It is an assault on a materialism which is seen as being at odds with human values, on a capitalist drive for profits which is inimical to the elaboration of an ethic based on the primacy of human life and the necessity to acknowledge a social contract. Indeed Joe Keller defends himself by insisting that his own values are those of the world in which he moves. As he asks, rhetorically, "Who worked for nothing in that war? When they work for nothing, I'll work for nothing. Did they ship a gun or a truck outa Detroit before they got their price? Is that clear? It's dollars and cents, nickels and dimes; war and peace, it's nickels and dimes, what's clear? Half the goddamn country is gotta go if I go." And his son is forced to acknowledge this, lamenting that "This is the land of the great big dogs, you don't love a man here, you eat him! That's the principle; the only one we live by—it just happened to kill a few people this time, that's all. The world's that way, how can I take it out on him?" Yet he still continues to press his demand of the ideal until his father can no longer live with his guilt and his suddenly intensified sense of loneliness. And this is the basis of the play's submerged theme—a concern with guilt as a principal mechanism of human behaviour, and with self-interest as a spectre behind the mask of idealism.

Clearly *All My Sons* rests very squarely on Ibsen's work, and in particular on *The Wild Duck*. This also had taken as its subject two businessmen, one of whom had allowed the weaker partner to go to prison for a fraud which he had himself condoned and probably initiated. He, like Joe Keller, had thrived as a consequence and, despite suspicions, won his way back into public regard. His son's suspicions cast a pall over his success and over his own imminent marriage which he hopes will finally expunge the memory of his first wife who had rightly accused him of betraying her. But Ibsen's emphasis is less on the relationship between father and son than it is on the nature of a supposed idealism itself. The son, Gregers Werle, is seized with what a benign doctor, Relling, calls "acute rectitudinal fever." He wishes to destroy all illusions in the belief that truth has a transcendent value, and that it provides the only basis for human life, but that idealism is seen to be an uneasy compound of guilt and naivety. In denying people their illusions he denies them also their life. And the consequence is the death of a young girl. But the play is by no means simply a defence of what Ibsen called "life-lies" and O'Neill "pipe dreams." Certain illusions are patently destructive, as is Greger's belief in his own innocence and his consequent assurance about the virtue of truth. Blind to his own self-deception, he becomes a huckster for truth at the expense of human values. In a world whose physical and moral boundaries are shrinking (the natural world has shrunk for the Ekdals to a simulated woodland recreated in their attic), those values become the crucial defence against material and physical constriction.

In Miller's play, too, there is an intricate tracery of self-justification. Most crucially, Chris's idealism conceals a compulsive need to justify his own silence, the suppression of his own doubts. The fact that he has refused to allow his father to add his name to that of the family firm is indicative of his own suspicions. Yet he has continued to draw money from the company. To accuse his father is, ultimately, to affirm his own innocence. So, too, his desire to force his mother to acknowledge his brother's death is less a consequence of his belief in the necessity for truth than a product of his desire to marry that brother's fiancée. Like so many of Miller's characters, his actions are dictated by his desire to "build something," even at the expense of others. Thus, his own repressed self-doubts about his involvement with business lead him to convince his doctor neighbour that he should abandon his practice for research. As a consequence the man leaves his wife for a while only to return with a brooding sense of dissatisfaction.

But Chris is not the only character whose actions are dictated by guilt. Joe Keller himself offers to help his partner and his son, as Ibsen's Werle had done in *The Wild Duck*. His wife struggles to maintain the fiction that her son is alive rather than admit to her husband's guilt and acknowledge her own status as a beneficiary of that crime. And, more crucially, Ann herself finally insists on showing both Joe and his wife their son's letter, partly in order to facilitate her own marriage and partly to purge her own sense of guilt. For she, like her brother, whose own concern with pressing the cause of justice is not remote from his own shame, has not visited or corresponded with her father since his imprisonment. To Joe Keller's appeal to "see it human" they all react in some fundamental way out of a need to justify themselves. The play is thus concerned with an egotism much more basic than that displayed by a materialistic society. This fact is identified but not examined. His characters move in a world of failed dreams; they are betrayed by time and event, desperately bending the world to accommodate their need for meaning and companionship. They see themselves as victims and struggle to find happiness and purpose in adapting themselves to the given. But Miller leaves us with only a series of paradoxes which are dramatised but not analysed. For in suggesting that all actions are rooted in self-concern he comes close to destroying the moral values which elsewhere he wishes to invoke. Morality is at one moment seen as external to individuals, who, deeply flawed, can scarcely elaborate a system of ethics which could only be an expression of that fallibility; at other times it is seen as being defined precisely in terms of the internal needs of those individuals, and hence subject to human imperfection. Morality as absolute; morality as relative.

The immorality of Joe Keller in forwarding defective goods is manifest, but his accusers can invoke no moral system by which to indict him, not because he inhabits a society in which such pragmatism is a norm but because there is no one in the play who can level the accusation without confessing to his or her own self-interest. It was a dilemma to which he would return in *After the Fall*, but in *All My Sons* not only does he not have an answer to the moral dilemma which he has created, he does not even seem fully aware of the nature of the problem which he has posed. For, if idealism and demands for justice must necessarily be flawed, on what grounds can any accusation be legitimately levelled? On the other hand, Chris's belief in human responsibility, reflected in the play's title and Joe Keller's final and dramatically crucial realisation that the pilots whom he indirectly killed were "all my sons," was born less out of this latter confession than out of an event in his own past, the loss of virtually all the members of his company during the war: "I got an idea—watching them go down. Everything was being destroyed, see, but it seemed to me that one new thing was made. A kind of responsibility. Man for man." But there is a suggestion that this too derives from guilt—the guilt of the survivor, for "They didn't die; they killed themselves for each other. I mean that exactly; a little more selfish and they'd've been here today." His survival thus becomes tinged with a suggestion of selfishness which is compounded by his subsequent financial security. "I felt wrong to be alive, to open the bank-book, to drive the new car, to see the new refrigerator." However the connection between idealism and guilt which he proposes is simply assumed; it is not traced to its origin in a model of human nature. In the earlier plays the impulse to transform the self and society had a purity denied here. Of course the war itself offers a potential explanation but the nature of the transformation which he implicitly proposes is not scrutinised. Some thirty years later Miller admitted to the significance of this submerged theme and to his fascination with the guilt of the idealist, but insisted that the sheer pressures of the moment, the immediate context of the war, made it impossible for this to break surface. Indeed he saw a similar logic behind the success, several decades after its first performance, of the Israeli production. The issue of war profiteering was simply too powerful in such an environment to permit more subtle and more disturbing questions to coalesce.

Both *The Wild Duck* and *All My Sons* end with a pistol shot. Gregers Werle remains undeflected from his destructive idealism; the dead girl's father seems likely to lapse back into his self-deceiving torpor. Only the doctor remains clear-sighted, aware of the constant battle between the real and the ideal. In *All My Sons* we are left with an irony which is worrying because Miller remains equivocal in his commitment to it. Thus a second before his father's suicide, Chris, who has precipitated that suicide, announces that "You can be better! Once and for all you can know there's a universe of people outside and you're responsible to it." In one sense this is clearly the moral of the play, but when the pistol shot rings out it is equally plain that his insistence on the moral has killed his father. When asked by his mother whether he was trying to kill his father with the truth, he had replied, "What was Larry to you? A stone that fell into the water? It's not enough for him to be sorry. Larry didn't kill himself to make you and Dad sorry." But seconds later, with his father dead, he says, "Mother, I didn't mean to." The equivocation is not merely Chris's, it is equally Miller's whose title announces *All My Sons* but whose play proposes an unbridgeable gulf between people and undercuts the very moral necessities he identifies. That contradiction could have become the basis for a more profound play. That it did not was perhaps an indication that the problem remained for him an intractable one until *After the Fall* in 1964, by which time he was clearer as to his view of human fallibility, personal betrayal and a continued commitment to the ideal, and less destabilised by the moral exigencies generated by the war.

All My Sons poses a further problem. It implies a critique of society and yet in effect identifies no way in which that society can be transformed. As Miller himself confessed more than thirty years later, "The argument that the Marxists had quite rightly, with that play, was that the son who brings down the wrath of the moral god, remains inside the system which has created this immorality. That's perfectly true. However, I believed then that with a sufficient amount of rigorousness those crimes could be resisted. It was a conviction which remained at the level of rhetoric. It never transformed itself into social action or dramatic effect. But Miller was less concerned with challenging the structure of American society than with revivifying a moribund liberalism, a capitalism purged only of its more evident rapacity.

All My Sons is a classically well-made play. With its concealed letters and hidden truths suddenly flourished at moments of dramatic effect, it recalls an earlier theatre. Its success plainly owed something to its topicality. Its melodramatic flavour reflected a public predilection for moral absolutes. Its resentments were those of the community at large who suspected, rightly enough, that profit rather than national interest had motivated many of those who risked capital rather than their lives. And, if there was, at another level, a profound ambiguity about the motives of those who flourished truth as a banner of their innocence, this had rather more to do with the play's literary origins in Ibsen than Miller's conscious concern with dissecting a certain failure at the heart of the liberal impulse. It is true that this would become increasingly important, but now the times seemed to demand some act of reconciliation, while the play's form, the very neatness of its construction, seemed to close the spaces against ambiguity, to deny that very moral incompletion which later became a principal subject of a writer for whom the social, the economic and the political increasingly seemed no more than symptoms of an imperfect human nature drawn equally to the delusive satisfactions of the self and the genuine transcendence of love.

For all its contemporary relevance, *All My Sons* was essentially a product of the 1930s. Its emphasis on human brotherhood, its thematic innocence and dramatic simplicities have rather more to do with the moral certainties and confident principles of pre-war and war-time America than the anxieties and existential dilemmas of the late 1940s and 1950s—a world of increasing material prosperity but of growing domestic and foreign paranoia. The success of communism abroad and fear of its subversive policies at home destabilised the political consensus and implicitly initiated a debate about those very American qualities and values which were presumably at stake. And, with the collapse of a consensus created originally by the economic necessities of the 1930s and the political requirements of war, individuals and groups felt themselves increasingly alienated. The assault on New Deal liberals, the barely concealed anti-Semitism of many of the attacks on supposed subversives, the distrust of intellectuals (associated in the minds of HUAC investigators, right-wing politicians and a number of industrialists, with a betrayal of American values) created a condition in which a writer like Miller was bound to find himself increasingly at odds with the model of America which that implied. The first evidence for this, apart from his novel, was *Death of a Salesman,* which placed the whole question of American values at the centre of his attention. And subsequently came *The Crucible,* which challenged head-on the corrupting influence of those who would enforce their own model of national purpose and personal morality on others. . . .

In the middle of Miller's notebook on *Death of a Salesman* he states his intention of writing "the Italian play," noting the case of "X., who ratted on the two immigrants." He then reminded himself that "the secret of the Greek drama is the vendetta, the family ties incomprehensible to Englishmen and Americans. But not to Jews. Much that has been interpreted in lofty terms, fate, religion, etc., is only blood and the tribal survival within the family. Red Hook is full of Greek tragedies."

A View from the Bridge, set in Red Hook, is his attempt at such a tragedy as well as his portrait of the informer, motivated, he suggests, by a compound of jealousy and guilt. Eddie Carbone, an Italian-American longshoreman, lives with his wife and niece, Catherine. His protective attitude towards that niece is not entirely free of a sexual desire which he can never acknowledge. But the situation is exacerbated by the arrival of two illegal immigrants, Marco and Rodolpho. When the latter forms a relationship with Catherine, Carbone does his best to destroy it, threatened in a way which he can barely understand. When everything else fails he calls the immigration department and turns informer. Challenged by Marco, he fights to uphold his name but is killed. While true to the original incident, which Miller had been told by a longshoreman, it was, however, consciously and ironically, false to the America of the mid 1950s, for it was not the informer but the man who refused to inform who found himself the social pariah. Indeed, in some senses *A View from the Bridge* offered a direct reversal of the situation described in *An Enemy of the People.* Stockmann finds himself reviled because he places truth and social well-being before self; Eddie Carbone is despised because he betrays that social bond out of a solipsistic desire to affirm his selfhood, to dominate his circumstances. Carbone is afraid of time and process. Refusing to recognise an aberrant impulse in himself he projects it onto others. The mechanism is thus the same as that which operates in *The Crucible.* The accuser denounces in others the sin which he suspects in himself.

Despite its power, the play lacks the weight of tragedy while Miller's concern with the betrayer threatens to lead to a disregard for those he betrays. Wife and niece's lover exist as dramatic statements rather than as complex individuals themselves, confused as to motivation and action. They have no inner life. Once again, though, his concern is with a moral failure, a failure to recognise normal human bonds. And, once again, sexual betrayal is at the heart of things. For Miller it clearly has an exemplary role. But the effect is to drain the act of its social meaning. Treachery which is a consequence of innate weakness, of an impulse which never rises into the rational world, can hardly become a component of Miller's moral dialectic. And Carbone's lack of control over his instincts is more absolute than Proctor's or Willy Loman's. For Proctor, it was one pole of a world rigidly constructed around the concrete war between good and evil. Surrender to irrationalism was a powerful attraction for a man uneasily located in a society which transforms morality into moralism, one for which charity and love are simple pieties and in which the effusion of passion is regarded as ethically and aesthetically reprobate. But for Eddie Carbone the world is otherwise. Certainly he denounces passion primarily because it is an image of the anarchy which he fears in his own being, but that passion is in his case literally misdirected. It is not simple adultery to which he is tempted, but a symbolic incest, since he acts as Catherine's father. He is anarchy incarnate. All his actions spill out of a central madness. And it is that madness which to some degree nullifies his force as a tragic hero and threatens his significance as social commentary. The play becomes less an analysis of the informer than a study of the madman, obsessive, self-destructive and destructive of others.

Like *The Crucible,* it was apparently conceived before the events which gave it its special social relevance, but it lacks what gave that play its particular force; it lacks self-conscious characters confronted with moral choices which are real because the alternatives which they face are equally available. Hence John Proctor had both challenged the authority of the church and submitted himself to it; both offered himself as putative leader and reneged on that offer. Thus, when presented with that choice again, complicated now by moral failings of a personal kind whose force he had acknowledged even while compounding them, and by the fact that the stakes are now his wife's and his own life as well as the lives of others, the options are real and have the force of past action behind them. For Eddie Carbone there is no choice. In terms of the character we are shown, he has no freedom of action. He is trapped in a moral system which is in fact no more than an aspect of his sexual compulsions. His actions certainly have no cultural or social function. He is pulled outside the society of man by an action which is not willed and therefore not inspected and has no social force. What he does in informing on two illegal immigrants who are also his wife's cousins, not to mention one of them being his niece's lover, is not illegal; it is simply presented as being immoral. And the authority for that view—which in a real social situation might actually be a fit subject for debate—lies in his own denunciation of such acts. But that denunciation has no force or application in his own case, for where there is no freedom there is no choice—where there is no choice there can be no culpability. It is not only a principle of natural law but a cause of fundamental significance to Miller's own moral view. Guilt cannot accrue by virtue of one's simple existence. That, after all, was too close to the position adopted by those for whom the Jew—placed in a position in which social action was severely circumscribed by law and prejudice—was forced to surrender his freedom of action and become guilty simply by enacting that determinism. It was the very position he had argued against in *Focus*. In *A View from the Bridge*, the loss of freedom, the presentation of action as simple pathology, not only undermines his moral point, it also erodes the play's theatrical potency. Once again it was to be a question to which he would return in *After the Fall*.

Miller's original version of the play, which was staged in September 1955, was a one-act verse drama deliberately pared down to essentials. As he explained:

> I saw the characters purely in terms of action . . . they are a kind of people who, when inactive, have no new significant definition as people. The form of the play, finally, had a special attraction for me because once the decision was made to tell it without an excess line, the play took a harder, more objective shape. In effect, the form announces in the first moments of the play that only that will be told which is cogent, and that this story is the only part of Eddie Carbone's life worth our notice and therefore no effort will be made to draw in elements of his life that are beneath these, the most tense and meaningful of his hours.

There seems a curious edge of contempt in Miller's description of his characters, a contempt at odds with his concern for the unique qualities of the self in its encounter with experience. His tragic aspirations seem to lead him to an external view of figures whose characters are subordinated to dramatic role.

Following a disappointing run, Miller reworked it for its London production. Much of the verse was refashioned as prose, the play became a two-act drama and character was rendered more densely. The effect was to root Carbone more securely in his setting, to move the play away from myth and towards a more substantial reality. But for all that it remains one of the less convincing of Miller's works. He himself thought that the changes which he had made did something to meet such objections. It is hard to agree. He explained the alterations, arguing that they led to a greater sympathy for his characters:

Perhaps the two most important were an altered attitude toward
Eddie Carbone, the hero, and toward the two women in his life.
I had originally conceived Eddie as a phenomenon, a rather
awesome fact of existence, and I had kept a certain distance from
involvement in his self-justification. Consequently, he had appeared as a kind of biological sport, and to a degree a repelling
figure not quite admissible into the human family. In revising the
play it became possible to accept for myself the implication I had
sought to make clear in the original version, which was that
however one might dislike this man, who does all sorts of frightful things, he possesses and exemplifies the wondrous and humane fact that he too can be driven to what in the last analysis
is a sacrifice of himself for his conception, however misguided, of
right, dignity and justice. In reversing it I found it possible to
move beyond contemplation of the man as a phenomenon into
an acceptance for dramatic purposes of his aims themselves.

This, Miller felt, had the effect of freeing the women characters, Eddie's wife
and niece, so that they could become more than simple observers. It also
"modified its original friezelike character" and the play, to Miller's mind,
moved closer to realism and became more engaged, more open to passion.
But his retention of Alfieri as narrator works against this, framing the action
as a conscious fable. Miller liked the more realistic setting which the play's
London director, Peter Brook, contrived, but that realism sits uneasily with
the myth-like qualities with which he had worked to invest Eddie Carbone.

It is a play about passion which is curiously drained of passion. Like so
many other of Miller's plays it is concerned with the implicit contract between people which proscribes betrayal, as it is with the individual's desperate need to maintain his own good opinion of himself. But in making
Eddie Carbone a victim of passion which he can neither articulate nor
acknowledge he deprives him of some ultimate responsibility for his own
actions. It is not that betrayal is rooted in self-interest, although viewed
objectively it is. It is that he acts under a compulsion which alienates him
from himself. He watches his own betrayal with a kind of detached horror
but feels unable to intervene. The lawyer/narrator Alfieri is the god to whom
he turns for absolution but in another sense he is simply an objectification
of his own tortured conscience. Unable to act, he wishes to see himself as the
unwilling victim of the gods. It is a central irony of the play that in some
sense Miller concedes this consolation by closing off Eddie's own self-
perception on all but the subconscious level. And when he confronts Marco

that self-deception, which is not willed but an expression of the degree to which his own motives have always been closed to him, brings him to the brink of madness. In defence of his honour he destroys the meaning of honour not merely in the sense that he is guilty of dishonourable actions but to the extent that Miller presents as psychopathology what might more appropriately have been seen as a tragic flaw. Eddie creates a fiction which will relieve him of responsibility but it is not a conscious invention. The play becomes in effect a psychological study of an individual who displaces his sexual passion into a concern with honour and family responsibility. In effect he resists the very analysis which is the basis of Miller's own dramatic strategy; that is he refuses to allow his motives to be stripped bare; he resists the process whereby his life is to be reduced to a simple passion. And if that is precisely the nature of the tragic dilemma it is nonetheless oddly at a tangent to Miller's own liberal theme, which is concerned to celebrate possibility, a freedom of action and thought at variance with the character of Carbone.

A *View from the Bridge* seems oddly external to Miller, and his decision to introduce a narrator through whom we see the events seems a natural objectification of this fact. It does convey something of that effect of a modern fable which he was anxious to achieve but it also withdraws our commitment. The play's virtues and vices are closely related. In a sense, the framing of the action is a deliberate strategy which has the effect of setting the events off as a legend, an exemplary tale, a tragic fiction, but it also subordinates character to tragic function and removes the action to a plane on which the logic of action seems, ironically, to have less to do with personal psychology than narrative necessity. Of course Eddie Carbone's dignity is that, unlike Alfieri, he will not settle for half. He offers total commitment in an age in which compromise is the order of the day. But it is a commitment to passion unregulated by morality. And there is a difference between the two versions of the play in this respect. The earlier verse drama emphasises the elemental power of the irrational side of the human animal, balanced in some respect by the rationality of Alfieri. The latter turns the play more in the direction of moral analysis. But in neither is there final conviction in so far as passion—by its nature intense, unsusceptible of analysis—is presented, for the most part, only as perverse (the love-affair between Catherine and Rodolpho is curiously passionless), while rationality is curiously impotent. For Alfieri, Eddie's distinction is that he allows himself to be wholly known and yet this, of course, is in no way willed. In so far as we glimpse his motive and commitment it is because we are allowed a perspective denied to the character. As a result it is hard to know what value to grant to the moral drama enacted before us. Is it simply that, like Willy Loman, he had all the wrong dreams and threw his life, his name and his passions behind a perverse phantom, or are we called upon to admire a man who breaks the code of his society in the name of some transcendent value whose authority is no less because it cannot be called by its proper name? Arguably, Eddie sacrifices his honour in order to save his honour. If his betrayal can be seen as being spawned by self-interest, it is possible to see it also as stemming from a desire to sustain the notion of innocence. Seen in this way he doesn't betray Rodolpho in order to gain Catherine for himself but to preserve her purity. If he is a rebel, it is not against a social code but the whole natural process which pulls the individual into an adult world in which betrayal, corruption and pride are the other side of maturity, sexual fulfilment and honour. His dignity and irony alike thus stem from his struggle to sustain a model of the world which is doomed to collapse. He becomes a kind of Dick Diver (in *Tender Is the Night*), deeply self-interested, but in a sense unable to stare into the darkness of his own motives because he is too busy trying to save others from a similar fate. In effect Eddie and Diver are linked by a willed collaboration in the anarchy that they seek to resist—an anarchy symbolised in Freudian terms by suggestions of incest. And yet both Miller and Fitzgerald clearly feel a certain admiration for someone who is willing to commit his whole being to sustain a fictional world in which the idea of innocence is preserved in the very midst of corruption.

Not the least of the ironies of the play is that Eddie Carbone's sin is to do his civic duty. Rodolpho is a law-breaker. But not for one moment does this seem of importance. Indeed Miller's social convictions are if anything expressed indirectly by his assumption that honour and justice are matters which exist at a tangent to the public world of law and civic responsibility. Values fundamentally derive from the need to respect oneself and others. The problem is that respect may be interpreted in different ways. Eddie's self-respect may be no more than pride or self-interest. But viewed differently it is, perhaps, rooted in his need to sustain a view of the world commensurate with his fantasies and dreams. If society has no right to generate prescriptive values, and if the self is deeply suspect, where are values born? It is a problem which *A View from the Bridge* raises but does not resolve.

Part of Eddie's problem is to have outlived his time, to be living at the wrong moment. His grand act, which would be an offence at any time, is nonetheless stripped of its grandeur and its glorious futility by its setting, a slum on the seaward side of the Brooklyn Bridge, described by Miller as "the gullet of New York." Miller, too, is not without his own nostalgia for a world in which something more than pragmatism and the daily urgencies of urban survival demand attention. His desire to create modern tragedies betokens as much, as does the pull of history in his work, implicit not simply in the historical setting of *The Crucible* but also in the longing for America's past which sounds, like Willy Loman's father's flute, through many of his plays. In a sense, his characters are as much destroyed by time as are Tennessee Williams's. They certainly all yearn for a past in which there had still been space—literal and metaphorical—for the moral conscience to function and, for a moment, perhaps a kind of adolescence, in which it was not necessary to acknowledge the reality and disabling pervasiveness of corruption. Yet as Miller seems to imply throughout his work, that very nostalgia might be the root of corruption. For, in play after play, the longing for innocence is not merely a symptom of its loss but the beginnings of an implacable evil. It is simply that it fails to break surface as an issue until *After the Fall* which, written, perhaps, to declare his innocence, turned into a confession of personal and social guilt.

A *View from the Bridge* appeared with *A Memory of Two Mondays*, which was itself a slight work related to its companion piece only by its use of verse. It was, in fact, often Miller's habit to write speeches in his notebooks in verse. Indeed it is this which in part explains his economy of language. But both of the plays in his double bill moved between verse and prose, two forms which correspond with Miller's dualism—his sense of human nature as a compromise or, more strictly, a sustained tension between spiritual yearning and physical enervation, between dream and prosaic reality. In *A View from the Bridge* Alfieri's lyrical invocations to human nature, his detached view of the unfolding of a naturally determined process, is close, perhaps too close, in spirit to that of Thornton Wilder's stage manager in *Our Town*. In *A Memory of Two Mondays*, the verse highlights a sense of nostalgia which has always been strong in Miller's work and which, in *Death of a Salesman*, constituted a real, if deceptive, source of value. Here, however, it relates only to a vaguely perceived sense of camaraderie ostensibly balanced by a realistic assertion of the need to subordinate human sensibilities to the exigencies of life. A minor work, *A Memory of Two Mondays* was a return to the world which Miller had known some ten years earlier.

Neither *The Crucible* nor *A View from the Bridge* was particularly successful with the public. *An Enemy of the People* was even less so, closing after thirty-six performances. Miller found himself increasingly at odds with his society. "From where I stood," he has recently said, "the country was going exactly one hundred and eighty degrees in the opposite direction. I didn't feel I had anything to say to these people. I really felt that I might as well be living in Zambia. I had absolutely no connection with these people any more." Asked whether he was, in effect, the figure in his film *The Misfits,* who sees the things he believes in being destroyed, he replied:

> Yes, I didn't see it that directly at the time, but yes ... It's not that it was difficult to relate; it was totally impossible. I felt that if they succeeded it would be a disaster for America and for the world ... There was no way to communicate and indeed we didn't communicate and I was left high and dry. Theater is a very public thing. You're not writing a poem for some small magazine.

Also he was confronted with a theatre structure which offered little outlet for drama beyond the Broadway theatre with which he was ethically and aesthetically at odds. He had, he explained,

> a sense that the whole thing wasn't worth the candle. Also the sense that the time had gotten away from me, that I didn't really understand or sympathize with what was going on here ... It all became rather pointless ... I wrote a lot of stuff and tore it up ... If I had had any kind of company of actors ... an active theater ... I probably would have written and completed a lot of stuff.

And it was, indeed, the emergence of Lincoln Center, rather than a fundamental shift in the mood of the American public, which eventually brought him back to the theatre after a nine-year silence. His despair of the Broadway audience might have been mitigated had he felt that he had any general support, but he felt that "I had been backed into a corner, really ... I didn't know who I was talking to." *The Misfits* showed him the possibility of appealing to a wider public, breaking through the barrier which he had felt growing around him. A comment on his alienation, it nonetheless played a role in terminating it. And he anyway detected a shift in American values. When President John F. Kennedy was elected, Miller was one of a clutch of writers, artists and scientists invited to his inauguration, though since his previous visits to Washington had been occasioned by subpoenas from the House Un-American Activities Committee, he was none too sure he could bring himself to go there without a lawyer. As he remarked, "I would naturally like to imagine that we are at the end of a period. To be perfectly blunt about it, I should call it the decade when America really got its brains knocked out. Indeed, I do not regard it as mere accident that the American Legion has recently taken to clubbing rabbits to death in wire enclosures. They have temporarily run out of intellectuals." Now, at least, it was possible that "a man capable of speaking and writing a complete English sentence will not for that reason alone be barred from public office." At last there was a return of confidence, but other more profound anxieties were about to surface in his work. . . .

For Miller, the Depression was a central experience. Not only had it shaped his own imagination and defined the terms of his own engagement with American values, but it was one of the few experiences genuinely shared by the American people as a whole. It provided the subject matter for his early unproduced and unpublished work; it prompted the political sympathies which, twenty years later, brought him before the House Un-American Activities Committee and, together with the events of the Second World War, it seems to have convinced him, on the one hand, of the fragility of personal identity and the social contract and, on the other, of the necessity to reaffirm the substance and significance of that identity and that contract. And if betrayal became a constant theme of his work, then it operated on a public no less than a private level. For the Miller who grew up in the 1930s the process of disillusionment, which is perhaps a natural part of the rites of passage from adolescence to maturity, coincided with a stripping of masks at a national level.

This also is essentially the process behind *The American Clock,* first produced at the Harold Clurman Theatre in New York City before opening at the Biltmore Theatre on November 20, 1980. Set in the 1930s and 1940s, it is an attempt to turn back "the American Clock . . . in search of those feelings that once ruled our lives and were stolen from us all by time." It is a familiar process in Miller's plays. The present contains the past while that past contains the clue to present behaviour. And *The American Clock* continues Miller's attempts to psychoanalyse America, to trace the origins of trauma. As he said in a speech to the Dramatists' Committee in 1956–57,

I used long ago to keep a book in which I would talk to myself. One of the aphorisms I wrote was, "The structure of a play is always the story of how the birds came home to roost." The hidden will be unveiled; the inner laws of reality will announce themselves; I was defining my impression of 1929 as well as dramatic structure.

The play in some senses comes full circle back to those early works submitted to the WPA in so far as it identifies in capitalism itself the source of a terrifying amorality. But where in those early plays he had been inclined to dramatise his capitalists as simple crooks and knowing exploiters of labour, now he is inclined to show them as baffled men, for the most part decent and without malice. They are as profoundly betrayed as those they have pulled along in their wake. The ideological certainty has disappeared. He offers brief portraits of petty officials anxious to capitalise on the situation but, for the most part, he seems concerned with offering a portrait of an America bewildered by the collapse of the dream.

A central figure, Lee, a young boy who seems to reflect something of Miller's own experiences of the Depression, is allowed to offer an analysis which would not have been remote from Miller's own at the time: "I keep trying to find the holes in Marxism but I can't. I just read an article where the salaries of twelve executives in the tobacco business was more than thirty thousand tobacco farmers made. That's what has happened—the workers never made enough to buy back what they produced. The boom of the Twenties was a gigantic fake. The rich have simply looted the people." But the prediction with which he concludes this analysis—"There is going to be a revolution"—deliberately undermines an analysis which, though reflecting accurately enough the instinctive radicalism of many at the time, remains at the level of rhetoric in the play as it did in the America of the 1930s.

The American Clock is in some respects a curious play. In a sense it is a pastiche of the attitudes and even the style of 1930s drama. In the original production some thirty-five parts were played by fifteen actors. These parts included financiers, farmers, a shoe-shine man, a prostitute, a seaman, and so on. In other words, it is a play which has epic pretensions, trying in some way to capture the mood of an entire society. But onto this is grafted, not entirely successfully, the story of a single family—the Baums. The collapse of their upper-middle-class life is offered as in some sense a paradigm of the disintegration of a central American myth—the prosperous immigrant family. Yet for all its offer to demythologise, to expose the fundamental betrayal of American values which he believes to have occurred in the 1920s and 1930s, it is a portrait which is still tainted with a certain residual nostalgia. The scenes that attempt to explore the poverty and need in the country at large remain, for the most part, at the level of assertion, brief agit-prop sketches which involve dispossession sales, and the feeding of a starving man with the milk from a baby's bottle (a less risqué version of the concluding scene of Steinbeck's *The Grapes of Wrath*). Those which concentrate on the Baum family show a group of people largely rising above their difficulties, displaying a resilience which seems not to be wholly unconnected with their apparent class superiority. There is, too, a certain smugness about the son's final speech which seems rooted less in his sensibility than in Miller's own liberal convictions. Thus, he observes that the Great Depression went down with the fleet at Pearl Harbour, "and with it, too, our resigned toleration of pointless suffering. Much was clarified by that blast." And, though he expresses uncertainty as to the reality of his mother's conviction "that the world was meant to be better," he confesses that "whenever I think of her . . . I always end up—with this headful of life!" The play ends with his mother at the piano uttering the single word, "Sing," as the stage directions indicate that "bright light flashes over the cloud-covered continent in the background." The end, in other words, directly mimics the conclusion of so many 1930s plays, most especially those of Clifford Odets. And it is difficult to resist the conclusion that *The American Clock* is Miller's attempt to pay his debt to the past.

It is the play which he never succeeded in getting produced in the 1930s, except that now he brings to it a kind of benediction which it is difficult to accept. Miller never wrote a play about Vietnam or the America so at odds with itself in the 1970s, unless it be *The Archbishop's Ceiling* which could perhaps be regarded as a response to the confusions and ambiguities of Watergate transposed to an East European setting. Instead, after his painful contemplation of the lessons of the war and the persecutions which followed it, he chooses to opt for nostalgia. *The American Clock* seems to have leapt back over such ambiguities to an era of clear issues in which character was unproblematic and rhetoric operated outside of the ironies which seem increasingly to have defined the nature of American experience. It is a hybrid play in several respects. It comes late in his career and has the air of a final gesture in its attempt at reconciliation, in its effort to lay the ghosts of the past and in the note of indulgent hope with which it concludes. Like Shakespeare's *The Tempest* it appears to offer a grace of sorts, to retreat some way from the extremes of human cruelty and self-betrayal, the moments of courage, of guilt, of anger and occasional despair which his plays forged into such potent images of a mid-twentieth-century world.

From the beginning of his career Arthur Miller has seen the individual being as deeply flawed but capable of resisting the fact of that imperfection.

In one sense he is a kind of reluctant Calvinist, believing in original sin but wishing to deny the determinism which that implies. In another sense he is a Freudian, seeing guilt as a basic mechanism of human behaviour. In yet another he is a confusing and confused blend of romantic radical and classic liberal, balancing the demands of the self against those of the group, seeing social behaviour as an expression of a fallible human nature, and announcing simultaneously the dignity, opacity and irreducible truth of personal identity and the human responsibilities which potentially render that identity suspect. In Miller's work nothing exists in pure form. Everywhere is division, tension without dialectic. Society becomes both a necessary protection against an imperfect human nature and an expression of it. The self is seen as the key to moral integrity and the source of a destructive egotism. And that is at the heart of a paradox which he could never satisfactorily resolve. For the will to pursue truth, to propound brotherhood, to propose a mutually supportive society of individuals constantly founders on his conviction of an ineradicable selfishness. The freedom which is required if moral principles are ever to be realised is denied by his acknowledgment of the implacable nature of history and human character. Time has an authority and defining power which makes it difficult to concede radical change. Ibsen, dominated by the past, can, when he chooses, slam the door on that past. He can conceive the individual as cutting a vector across the social world. For Miller that past cannot be so easily denied, except in his very first plays which positively glow with a belief in the transformation of the self and society. But in the post-war plays, with the possible exception of *All My Sons* (and even here the ideal is stained with guilt and self-interest), no Miller protagonist believes, as does Ibsen's Stockmann, that the individual can successfully challenge history and the public world. They all grant its implacable nature and try to win what battles they may within its contours. Miller wishes to believe in certain fundamental moral truths. Ibsen is less sure. Miller's decision to omit Stockmann's claim, that "There is no established truth that can remain true for more than seventeen, eighteen at most twenty years," is crucial. For Miller, if that were accepted as an adequate description of reality, the moral axes of his world would collapse.

And this is why he has tended to regard his work as tragic. The crucial victory won by his characters is a private one. The struggle is to sustain one's integrity in what is accepted as a determined world. The problem is that in the early plays the rhetoric in fact suggests otherwise. It proposes the possibility of transforming society. It announces the need for a complete transformation of the social system in such a way that the individual conscience will be able to operate but can propose no way in which that transformation can be effected.

Miller's central theme is the problem of relating one's deeds to one's conception of oneself. The echoic insistence on identity, the endlessly repeated demands to sustain one's name in the face of flux and in the teeth of personal betrayal, suggests a Platonic sense of self which must be maintained. It is the correlative of that idealism, of spiritual fulfilment, which even the least articulate of his protagonists requires in order to continue living. But that absolute need to insist on one's innocence repeatedly finds itself in conflict with an imperfect human nature and a deterministic world. It is a tension which Biff Loman and John Proctor recognise, in *Death of a Salesman* and *The Crucible* respectively, and from which they derive a true sense of being. It is a tension which Willy Loman and Eddie Carbone, in *Death of a Salesman* and *A View from the Bridge,* refuse to acknowledge. As a consequence they remain locked inside their own illusions, condemned to the inner solitariness which is the result of a failure of self-knowledge. With the later plays that innocence is seen as a fantasy and the need to insist on its reality the root of human cruelty.

Miller identifies his persistent assertion of the necessity to struggle with determining realities as rooted in both his Jewish and American identity. He has said that the Jewish element is important not only in his work but in that of a number of American writers, because the Jew cannot afford to flirt with apocalypse, cannot "exult in disaster, because the elimination of the Jew is a credible proposition, it is one with an historical reality to it." Consequently, "the grip on life, the demand that life continue, is very close to the surface." And this, he sees, as equally strong in America. His work, in one form or another, is thus a search for the basis on which life may be continued, on which imperfection may be accepted as an undeniable but not disabling truth.

In recent years Miller's reputation has been somewhat eclipsed. He no longer seems to address the immediate moral problems of the age as once he did. Perhaps this is because, as Susan Sontag remarked in her essay "Going to the Theatre, etc.," "We still tend to choose our images of virtue from among our victims," but "in just a few short years the old liberalism, whose archetypal figure was the Jew, has been challenged by the new militancy, whose hero is the Negro." Certainly in the 1960s and early 1970s what seemed the passive acceptance at the heart of *After the Fall* and *The Price,* and even, in a sense, of *Incident at Vichy* was at odds with the new orthodoxy. Certainly it is also true that Miller never really challenged the essential premises of his society in such a way as to suggest the necessity for or the possibility of radical change. He seemed only to advocate a kind of moralised capitalism, a return to the liberal virtues of a pre-urban New England. But he was never really a political radical. His chief struggle as an artist and as a public figure was to reinvest the individual with a moral responsibility apparently stripped from him by economic determinism and the forces of history. He believed and believes still in the social contract. But he has seen it abrogated too frequently and too profoundly to believe it to be anything but fragile and contingent. The purpose and process of his plays has thus been to locate the individual in a social context which goes some way to explain but never wholly to define his or her identity. The dominant image of his plays is of that individual in relationship to family and society, and if from the very beginning he felt that betrayal was a natural compulsion he has also continued to insist that there is a counterforce which seeks to heal the wounds, to find the meaning of the self beyond the self. If the space available for action is ever diminishing, as the city closes in on the individual and the walls of the prison cell cast their shadow, in the darkness there remains a crucial spirit of resistance. And the heart of that resistance is the imagination, which is still capable of projecting itself into the place and the sensibility of the other. And since that is the method of drama the theatre itself becomes both an image and an example of this process.

As he said in a speech made in the late 1950s:

> You can't understand anything unless you understand its relationship to its context. That much, for good [or] ill, the Great Depression taught me. It made me impatient with anything, including art, which pretends that it can exist for its own sake and still be of any importance. A thing becomes beautiful to me as it becomes internally and externally organic. It becomes beautiful because it removes some of my helplessness before the chaos of experience. I think one of the reasons I became a playwright was that in dramatic form everything must be gently organic, deeply organized, articulated from a living center.

Art becomes a principal means of exposing a hidden process and hence the basis of a reassurance about the nature of experience. Outside the pure blank face of evil, which remains inscrutable to him, all experience, public and private, was available for examination and could be explained and understood by means of rational analysis. It was a lesson which he felt himself to have learned from Freud no less than Marx, from liberal philosophy no less than from writers like Dostoyevski and Ibsen. As he said of the latter:

I connected with Ibsen not because he wrote about problems, but because he was illuminating process . . . From his work, read again and again with new wonders cropping up each time, as well as through Dostoyevski's, I came to an idea of what a writer was supposed to be. These two issued the license, so to speak, the only legitimate one I could conceive, for presuming to write at all. One had the right to write because other people needed news of the inner world, and if they went too long without such news they would go mad with the chaos of their lives. With the greatest of presumption I conceived that the great writer was the destroyer of chaos, a man privy to the councils of the hidden gods who administer the hidden laws that bind us all and destroy us if we do not know them. And chaos, for one thing, was life lived oblivious of history.

As time went on, a lot of time, it became clear to me that I was not only reporting to others but to myself first and foremost. I wrote not only to find a way into the world but to hold it away from me so that it would not devour me.

There is a fragment of a play in one of Miller's notebooks at the University of Texas in which a writer looks back over his life. It is so close to his own experience as to suggest that it is a self-portrait. It certainly describes a process which is reflected in his plays from the earliest work through to the deeper anxieties and insecurities of the work that he produced in the 1960s and 1970s:

Sometimes I think it's only that I'm suffering because socialism collapsed as an ideal. Sometimes it seems as though we had a peculiar advantage, growing up in the Depression. As bad as it got there was always a kind of promise in the air—people seemed on the way to being good. We were supposed to be such hardheaded materialists, now I think we were really the last of a long line of romantics. Everybody could be saved if only society were just and prosperous. It didn't matter how good or bad a person was—only what he believed. There's no belief any more.

As he said in 1979, the moral world has been under increasing pressure throughout his work:

but I've been struggling with it, you see. Anyway, I think the struggle is necessary. When the struggle is given up (and it is really given up in totalitarian places) then we're all up for grabs and I'm not ready to give up . . . You've got to grapple with this somehow. It seems insane to say this, and maybe I've lived here too long in this district, in New England, but I believe there is an appeal to people left. You have to work at it but you can make it, and this is a democracy here, you see. I'm not so sure I would feel this way if I lived in the middle of New York City where I was born, you see? But this is as real as that, isn't it? I mean, this is taking place. This is not a delusion in my mind. See, these people here in their blundering, in our blundering, sometimes completely mistaken way, once they get a glimmer of some path, can make it happen within certain tenets but they are very broad tenets . . . My effect, my energy, my aesthetic lies in finding the chain of moral being in the world . . . somehow.

The theatre is a crucial mechanism in this search. After the production of *All My Sons* it seemed to him that the stage itself was "as wide and free and towering and laughingly inventive as the human mind itself." And if that sense of freedom has been attenuated, if that sense of physical and moral space has been drastically curtailed, the imagination still survives. The social act which is both a necessary precondition for theatre and the basis of its method is itself an assertion of value. It is a model of that sense of human community which has been threatened but not, in Miller's eyes, destroyed by a fallible human nature and the history to which that human nature has given birth. To Miller, the imagination is a value and the theatre a testament to the human need to understand, to communicate and to create a reality which we can inhabit with dignity and hope.

In the introduction to his *Collected Plays,* Miller insisted that determinism, whether it was based on the "iron necessities" of economics or psychoanalytic theory, "is a contradiction of the idea of drama itself," because it leaves out of account "an innate value, an innate will [which] does in fact posit itself as real not alone because it is devoutly to be wished, but because, however closely he is measured and systematically accounted for, he is more than the sum of his stimuli and is unpredictable beyond a certain point." To him, drama exists precisely to show this moment of transcendence, to attempt to explore the nexus between determinism and free will. And while his confidence has undoubtedly leached away over the years his own summary of his work can still stand. His plays, he insisted, were all ultimately dedicated to the faith that, just as a play is more than the sum of its parts, "we are made and yet we are more than what made us."

No other American dramatist has so directly engaged the anxieties and fears, the myths and dreams, of a people desperate to believe in a freedom for which they see ever less evidence. No other American writer has so successfully touched a nerve of the national consciousness. But Miller is claimed with equal avidity by the international community. *The Crucible* was seen by the Chinese as immediately relevant to a cultural revolution in which youth had exacted its revenge on an adult world. *Death of a Salesman* has been hailed in countries where the profession itself is unknown. Miller may have been moved to write by specific circumstances but the plays which resulted transcended those circumstances as they did national boundaries. He is, above all, a writer whose art and example have dignified the theatre which for him has always been a realm of possibility, a paradigm of that tension between the given and the created within which we all move and have our being.

E. MILLER BUDICK

History and Other Spectres
in The Crucible

In his *Defense of Historical Literature*, David Levin has argued that Arthur Miller's *The Crucible* fails to achieve artistic profundity because of Miller's inability to project seventeenth-century sensibilities and thus to sympathize with them. The play, in Levin's view, and in the views of many other critics as well, is not seriously historical and, therefore, not seriously literary or political. "Mr. Miller's pedagogical intention," writes Levin, "leads him into historical and, I believe, aesthetic error. . . . Since Mr. Miller calls the play an attack on black-or-white thinking, it is unfortunate that the play itself aligns a group of heroes against a group of villains." Levin concludes his discussion with the observation that "stupid or vicious men's errors can be appalling; but the lesson would be even more appalling if one realized that intelligent men, who tried to be fair and saw the dangers in some of their methods, reached the same conclusions and enforced the same penalties." Miller's *Crucible*, it would seem, fails to reach the social, historical, and (therefore) moral depth of a great work of art, because it cannot imaginatively conjure the world that it pretends to describe.

And yet, as Cushing Strout has pointed out, "Miller has argued for [the] historical truth [of the play], pointed to its contemporary parallels, and defined its transhistorical subject as a social process that includes, but also transcends, the Salem witchcraft trials and the anticommunist investigations of the 1950s." Furthermore, Miller has declared that the Salem witchcraft trials, which form the central action of the drama, were of interest to him

From *Modern Drama* 28, no. 4 (December 1985). © 1985 by University of Toronto, Graduate Centre for the Study of Drama.

long before he confronted McCarthyism and decided to write a play impli-
cating the country's contemporary hysteria. How historically accurate, then,
is Miller's play? And what are we to make of its use of historical materials,
both past and present?

Though *The Crucible* is, to be sure, unrelenting in its opposition to the
authoritarian systems represented by Puritanism and McCarthyism, its use
of historical materials and the position on moral tyranny which it thus
projects seem to me far more complex than criticism on the play would
suggest. For Miller's play is not interested only in proclaiming a moral
verdict, either on historical or on contemporary events. It does not want
simply to inculcate a moral by analogizing between past experiences, on
which we have already reached a consensus, and contemporary problems,
from which we may not have the distance to judge. Indeed, as Miller himself
has stated, while "life does provide some sound analogies now and again, . . .
I don't think they are any good on the stage. Before a play can be 'about'
something else, it has to be about itself." Analogizing, then, is not, I think,
either the major subject of the play or its major structural device. Rather,
The Crucible is concerned, as Miller has claimed it is, with clarifying the
"tragic process underlying the political manifestation," and, equally important, with describing the role of historical consciousness and memory in
understanding and affecting such a process.

History is not simply a device which Miller employs in order to escape
the unmediated closeness of contemporary events. Rather, it is a fully developed subject within the play itself. For history is for Miller precisely what
enables us to resist the demon of moral absolutism. As Miller himself puts
it [in his introduction to *Collected Plays*]:

> It was not only the rise of "McCarthyism" that moved me, but
> something which seemed much more weird and mysterious. It
> was the fact that a political, objective, knowledgeable campaign
> from the far Right was capable of creating not only a terror, but
> a new subjective reality, a veritable mystique which was gradu-
> ally assuming even a holy resonance. . . . It was as though the
> whole country had been born anew, without a memory even of
> certain elemental decencies which a year or two earlier no one
> would have imagined could be altered, let alone forgotten.

It is this "subjective reality," and the problem of "memory," that are, I
believe, at the heart of Miller's play. And for this reason Miller turns to the
Puritan Americans for his subject. For the Salem witch trials raised supremely well the same terror of a "subjective reality" metamorphosing into

a "holy resonance" and assuming an objective truth. Indeed, in one sense, this is what the controversy of spectre evidence was all about. Furthermore, the re-creating of this "subjective reality" in the equally "subjective reality" of a drama representing both history and literature—themselves two versions of reality created by the human imagination—directly confronts the relationship of the subjective and the objective, and provides a model for mediating between the two, a model which has at its centre the very issue of memory which is also of paramount importance to Miller. Whether by intuition or by intention, "the playwriting part" of Miller digs down to the essential historical issues of the period as the historians themselves have defined them—issues such as spectral evidence, innate depravity, and its paradoxical corollary, visible sanctity—and relates these issues to the problem of human imagination and will.

Like so much historical fiction and drama, *The Crucible* forces a revolution in our perception and definition of reality. It causes what appears to us to be immediate and real—the present—to become dreamlike and subjective, while it enables what we assume to be the less stable aspects of our knowledge—the ghosts of the past—to assume a solidity they do not normally possess. As Miller says of his own relationship to the Salem of his play, "Rebecca, John Proctor, George Jacobs—[these] people [were] more real to me than the living can ever be"; the "only Salem there ever was for me [was] the 1692 Salem." The past for Miller is "real." Conversely, the subject of his play, the guilt which characterizes both Proctor and, by implication, many of the victims of McCarthyism, is an "illusion" which people only mistake for "real." What could be closer to the spirit of the Salem witch trials, in which people mistook illusions of guilt and sinfulness for "real" witches; in which they assumed a necessary correlation between inner goodness and outward manifestations of that grace? Guilt, writes Miller, is the "betrayer, as possibly the most real of our illusions." "Nevertheless," he continues, it is "a quality of mind capable of being overthrown." If Miller's play intends to be revolutionary, it is in terms of this psychological revolution that it expresses itself.

Miller's play, we would all agree, is an argument in favour of moral flexibility. The fundamental flaw in the natures of the Puritan elders and by extension of the McCarthyites, as Miller sees it, is precisely their extreme tendency toward moral absolutism. "You must understand," says Danforth, "that a person is either with this court or he must be counted against it, there be no road between." But Miller is interested, not only in establishing the fact of such absolutism and condemning it, but also in isolating the factors which cause the rigidity which he finds so dangerous. And he is anxious to propose avenues of escape from the power of an over-active, absolutizing moral conscience. As we have seen, critics have objected to Miller's apparently one-sided moralizing in the play. But this moralizing, we must note, is concentrated almost exclusively in the prologue introductions to characters and scenes, and these narrative intrusions into the action of the play may no more represent Miller, the playwright, than Gulliver represents Jonathan Swift or Huck Finn, Mark Twain. Indeed, as other critics have pointed out, the play proper portrays a remarkably well-balanced community of saints and sinners which deserves our full attention and sympathy. Despite the annoying persistence of such unmitigated villainy as that represented by judges Danforth and Hathorne, there is moral education in the course of the drama (in Hale and Parris), while throughout the play such characters as Goody Nurse and Giles Corey represent unabated moral sanity and good will. Furthermore, John Proctor, the opponent of all that seems evil in the play, is not an uncomplicated hero. If we put aside for a moment Proctor's indiscretion with Abigail Williams, which itself has serious social, not to mention ethical, implications, Proctor, who has not taken his sons to be baptized, who does not appear regularly in church (all because of a personal dislike for the appointed representative of the church), and who does not respect Puritan authority even before the abhorrent abuse of power during the trials, does represent, if not an enemy, then at least a potential threat to a community which, Miller is quick to acknowledge, is involved in a life-death struggle to survive.

In fact, it is in the ambiguous nature of the play's hero and his relationship to the rest of the community that Miller begins to confront the complexity of the work's major issue. For if the Salem judges suffer from an unabidable moral arrogance, so does John Proctor, and so, for that matter, do many other of the play's characters. *The Crucible* is a play seething with moral judgements on all sides, on the parts of its goodmen (and goodwomen) as well as of its leaders. The courts condemn the "witches," to be sure, and this act is the most flagrant example of over-zealous righteousness in the play. But the Proctors and their friends are also very free in their moral pronouncements (note the otherwise exemplary Rebecca's much resented *"note of moral superiority"* in act 1), as is Miller's own narrator, who, as we have already observed, is totally unselfconscious in his analyses of his Puritan forbears' ethical deficiencies. The point, I think, is that moral arrogance, the tendency to render unyielding judgments, is not confined within the American power structure. It is at the very heart of the American temperament, and therefore it is at the heart of Miller's play as well. For *The Crucible* attempts to isolate the sources of moral arrogance, to determine the psychological and perceptual distortions which it represents, and thus to point the direction to correcting our moral optics.

Obviously John Proctor does not represent the same threat to freedom posed by Danforth and Hathorne. But this may be the point exactly, that Proctor does not possess the power, the authority, which converts stubbornness, arrogance, guilt, and pride into social dangers. We must remember, however, that neither did the Puritans wield such dangerous authority until after they had ascended to power in the new world. The story of Proctor, therefore, may be in part the story of American Puritanism itself, Puritanism which wrestled with its own sense of original sin and damnation, which overcame enemies like the Anglican Church which would judge and persecute it, and which finally fought to establish the pure church, the church of the individual saints, in America. Proctor fails in his struggle against persecution of conscience. The Puritan church succeeded—but only for a time. Indeed, this apparent difference between Proctor and the Puritans serves only to stress how corrupting power can become in the hands of a certain kind of person, the Puritan American who is obsessed by his own guilt and driven by the desire to determine sanctity in himself and in others, and to make it conform to the visible human being.

As Miller himself states, guilt is a major force behind and throughout his drama. The major action of the play revolves, therefore, not around the courts and their oppression of the community (the natural analogue to the McCarthy trials), but rather around the figure of Miller's goodman, John Proctor. Miller's real interest resides neither in the sin of tyranny (the courts) nor in the crime of subversion (Proctor's rebellion from authority), but in the sources of tyranny and rebellion both, and in the metaphysical (or religious) assumptions and psychological pressures which cause individuals to persecute and be persecuted for arbitrarily defined crimes of conscience. The personal history of Proctor is the very best kind of history of the Puritan theocracy, just as the story of the Puritans is the very best kind of history of America itself, for both stories probe to the roots, not only of a community, but of the very mentality which determined that community. It is a most powerful irony of the play that Proctor is victimized and destroyed by the very forces which, despite his apparent opposition, he himself embodies. The witch trials do, as Miller says in his "Echoes Down the Corridor," break "the power of theocracy in Massachusetts." But the seeds of this destruction were less within the chimerical crime of witchcraft than within the rigours of the Puritan definition of sainthood which identified moral goodness with outward manifestations of salvation, a belief which, as we shall see momentarily, characterized "witches" and judges alike. For, as the

Puritans themselves came to recognize, the implications of spectre evidence, the realization that the devil could assume the person of a child of light, essentially undermined the Puritans' conviction in visible sanctity and hence in the possibility of a federal community predicated upon such sanctity. If devils could parade as saints, how could one determine who in fact was saved, who damned? The danger which Miller sees for his contemporary American public is not that it will fail to recognize totalitarianism in the Puritans, or even in McCarthy. Totalitarianism is too easy an enemy, as the McCarthy phenomenon itself demonstrates in its hysterical reaction to Communism. The danger is that the Americans will not be able to acknowledge the extent to which tyranny is an almost inevitable consequence of moral pride, and that moral pride is part and parcel of an American way of seeing the world, an aspect of the tendency to externalize spiritual phenomena and claim them as absolute and objective marks of personal or political grace.

The major historical fabrication of the play is, of course, the adulterous relationship between Proctor and Abigail Williams. Many explanations have been offered for this alteration of the historical facts (Miller himself comments on it), but the chief necessity for inventing this adultery is, I think, that it provides precisely that inclination to perceive oneself as sinful, as innately depraved, which characterizes both Proctor and the Puritans, and which therefore delineates that field of ambiguous moral constitution in which both the individual and his community must define and measure moral "goodness." Proctor's adultery with Abigail establishes the hero a fallen man, fallen even before the action of the play begins. This may not be original sin as the Puritans defined it, but it is a sin which is prior and unrelated to the specific sin which the play explores, the covenanting of oneself to the devil, or, to put the problem in the more secular terminology that Miller would probably prefer, to the pursuing of a course of consummate, antisocial evil.

The question being raised in Miller's play is this: on what basis can an individual exonerate himself of evil, knowing that he is indeed sinful and that according to his own beliefs he is damned? To put the question somewhat differently: how can John Proctor or any man believe in his own possible redemption, knowing what he does about the nature of his sexual, sinful soul? Our distance from Proctor's dilemma may enable us to understand levels of complexity which Proctor cannot begin to acknowledge. But this does not alter in the least the conflict which he must resolve. Nor does it protect us from analogous complexities in our own situations which we do not have the distance to recognize. Indeed, as Miller himself argues, "guilt" of the vague variety associated with Proctor, was directly responsible for the "social compliance" which resulted in McCarthy's reign of terror in the 1950s: "Social compliance . . . is the result of the sense of guilt which individuals strive to conceal by complying. . . . It was a guilt, in this historic sense, resulting from their awareness that they were not as Rightist as people were supposed to be." Substituting "righteous" for Rightist, one has a comment equally valid for the Puritans.

Puritan theology, to be sure, had its own sophisticated answers to the question of the sinner's redemption. According to the Puritan church, the crucifixion of Christ represented the final act of reconciliation between man and God after man's disobedience in the garden of Eden had rent their relationship asunder. God in His infinite mercy chose to bestow upon certain individuals his covenant of grace, and thus to bring them, sinful as they might be, back into the congregation of the elect. God's will, in the process of election, was total, free, and inscrutable. Human beings were passive recipients of a gift substantially better than anything they deserved. This theological position is hinted at in the play when Hale pleads with Elizabeth Proctor to extract a confession from her husband:

> It is a mistaken law that leads you to sacrifice. Life, woman, life is God's most precious gift; no principle, however glorious, may justify the taking of it. . . . Quail not before God's judgment in this, for it may well be God damns a liar less than he that throws his life away for pride.

Miller has secularized and diluted Puritan theology in Hale's speech, but the references to "sacrifice," "judgment," and "pride" suggest the outlines of Christian history from the Puritan perspective, and they point to the central fact that divine charity has made human sacrifice unnecessary, even presumptuous, in the light of the divine sacrifice which has already redeemed humankind.

But, as we shall see in a moment, factors other than the covenant of grace had entered into the Puritans' religious views, forcing a conflict already evident in the first generation of New Englanders, and threatening to tear the community apart by 1660, between a strict Calvinism on the one hand and a federal theology on the other. This conflict was essentially a competition between the covenant of grace, which emphasized the charity implicit in Christ's crucifixion, and the covenants of church and state, which were essential to the Puritans' political objectives and which manifested themselves as legal contracts designed to forge an identity between inner grace and outer saintliness. In other words, in demanding outward obedience to the federal form of government which they had conceived for their "city upon a hill," the organizers of the new community of saints had hedged on their Calvinism; they had muted the doctrine of the absoluteness of the covenant of grace, the ineffectiveness of signs to evidence justification, in order to assert the importance of social conformity, of "preparation," and of an external obedience to the covenant, not of grace, but of church and state.

From one point of view, the tragedy of John Proctor, which culminates in his execution for witchcraft, can be seen as stemming from his and his wife's inability to relent in their own moral verdicts, both of themselves and of each other, and to forgive themselves for being human. It originates, in other words, in their failure to understand the concept of divine charity which has effected their salvation and saved them from damnation. "I am a covenanted Christian woman," Elizabeth says of herself, but neither she nor John seems to understand what this covenant of grace means. Like the Puritan community of which they are a part, they seem to feel compelled personally to exact from themselves justice and to punish themselves for the sinfulness for which Christ's crucifixion has already atoned.

Not understanding the model of divine charity which determines their sanctity, they and their fellow Puritans are incapable of understanding the concept of charity at all. True, they plead charity. "We must all love each other now," exclaims Mary Warren in act 2. "Excellency," pleads Hale, "if you postpone a week and publish to the town that you are striving for their confessions, that speak mercy on your part, not faltering." "You cannot break charity with your minister," Rebecca cautions John; "Learn charity, woman," Proctor begs Elizabeth; "Charity Proctor, charity" asks Hale; "I have broke charity with the woman, I have broke charity with her," says Giles Corey. But even as they beg for mercy and sympathy, charity in the largest, most theologically meaningful sense of the word, they act in accordance, not with charity, but with that other component of the divine will—justice—which God has specifically chosen not to express by substituting the covenant of grace for His justifiable wrath. Thus, in the name of justice, Parris forces a confession from Abigail, Hale from Tituba; Abigail threatens Betty and the other girls; Proctor (significantly) does not *ask* Mary Warren to tell the truth but demands it of her, and so on. We know we are in terrible trouble when Hale, upon hearing of Rebecca's arrest, pleads with her husband to "rest upon the justice of the court." Justice alone simply will not do. Indeed, when justice forgets charity, it subverts the whole divine scheme of salvation, as the Puritans' theology had itself defined it.

Miller uses the issues of charity and justice both in order to locate the historical controversy which destroyed Salem, Massachusetts, and to develop an argument concerning the relationship between charity and justice as theological concepts, and charity and justice as the major features of human relationships—public and private. These issues, therefore, not only frame the play, but specifically define the relationship between John and Elizabeth Proctor, and they largely determine the course of their tragedy. In John and Elizabeth's first extended conversation, set in the "court" which is the Proctors' home, a play in miniature is enacted, a dramatic confrontation which explores the same issues of charity and justice portrayed in the play as a whole:

PROCTOR: Woman . . . I'll not have your suspicion any more.

ELIZABETH: . . . *I* have no—

PROCTOR: I'll not have it!

ELIZABETH: Then let you not earn it.

PROCTOR, *with a violent undertone*: You doubt me yet?

ELIZABETH, *with a smile, to keep her dignity*: John, if it were not Abigail that you must go to hurt, would you falter now? I think not. . . .

PROCTOR, *with solemn warning*: You will not judge me more, Elizabeth. I have good reason to think before I charge fraud on Abigail, and I will think on it. Let you look to your own improvement before you go to judge your husband any more. . . . Spare me! You forget nothin' and forgive nothin'. Learn charity, woman. I have gone tiptoe in this house all seven month since she is gone. I have not moved from there to there without I think to please you, and still an everlasting funeral marches round your heart. I cannot speak but I am doubted, every moment judged for lies, as though I come into a court when I come into this house! . . . I'll plead my honesty no more. . . . No more! I should have roared you down when first you told me your suspicion. But I wilted, and, like a Christian, I confessed. Confessed! Some dream I had must have mistaken you for God that day. But you're not, you're not, and let you remember it! Let you look sometimes for the goodness in me, and judge me not.

ELIZABETH: I do not judge you. The magistrate sits in your heart that judges you. I never thought you but a good man, John— *with a smile*—only somewhat bewildered.

PROCTOR, *laughing bitterly*: Oh, Elizabeth, your justice would freeze beer! *He turns suddenly toward a sound outside. He starts for the door as Mary Warren enters. As soon as he sees her, he goes directly to her and grabs her by her cloak, furious.* How do you go to Salem when I forbid it? do you mock me? *Shaking her.* I'll whip you if you dare leave this house again!

What is important in this scene is not just that Elizabeth's lack of charity toward John leads directly to Proctor's lack of charity both toward Elizabeth and toward Mary Warren as she enters the house; or that this cycle of anger and recrimination causes further hostility on the parts of the two women who hold each other's and John's fate in their hands. (An analogous kind of reading could be made for John's confrontation with Abigail earlier in the play, when John not only fails to respond to Abigail's very real and understandable hurt ["Pity me, pity me!", she pleads], but absolutely refuses even to acknowledge that the affair ever occurred: "PROCTOR: Wipe it out of mind. We never touched, Abby. ABIGAIL: Aye, but we did. PROCTOR: Aye, but we did not." The point is not simply that anger begets anger, nor that the characters do not trust each other. Rather, the problem is that the characters have not admitted humankind's very paltry powers of moral judgement. They have not accepted in their hearts that God alone can render judgement on humankind. The characters of the play—*all* the characters, and not just Danforth and Hathorne—have mistaken themselves for God, to paraphrase Proctor, and this misunderstanding is precisely the problem. Elizabeth cannot see the "goodness" in John just as she cannot see the "goodness" in herself (and John, later, cannot see the "goodness" in himself), because what both John and Elizabeth have forgotten is that, according to their own beliefs, the goodness within them is not a natural goodness but the goodness implanted there by God's grace, despite the fact that they are, to apply Elizabeth's own words about herself, "so plain" and "so poorly made." We can expand the argument by pointing out John and Elizabeth's unwillingness to recognize that goodness is not contingent upon a single action or even upon a series of actions. Goodness does not depend upon what the Puritans would call "works." Rather, goodness is an indwelling potentiality—whether innate, for the secularists, or implanted there by God—which must be nurtured and allowed to express itself. On a larger theological scale, the fundamental problem for both John and Elizabeth is a lack of faith in a true sense, a failure to recall their religion telling them that God has saved them *despite* the fact that they are sinners, and that the means of their salvation was divine charity itself.

This playing out of the drama's theological issues as a conflict between a guilty adulterer and his suspicious wife serves supremely well Miller's ultimate object of "examining . . . the conflict between a man's raw deeds and his conception of himself; the question of whether conscience is in fact an organic part of the human being, and what happens when it is handed over not merely to the state or the mores of the time but to one's friend or wife." The Puritan Proctor could not have provided a fitter subject for the study of the organicism of conscience, because for the Puritans inner grace and outer obedience to the "state" and to the "mores of the time" had become hopelessly confused. Goodness had lost its theological meaning and degenerated into a merely human concept. Hence, to the end of the play neither Elizabeth nor John fully understands the meaning of the word "goodness," although Hale, again in an abbreviated and somewhat debased form, gives a basis for the theological definition when he tells us in the fourth act that "before the laws of God we are as swine." The point is valid, despite the somewhat crude and objectionable formulation. Yet, even though in the final act of the play Elizabeth knows that she "cannot judge" Proctor, especially not his goodness, and even though Proctor has again and again reiterated that he and his goodness cannot be judged either by Elizabeth or by the courts, Elizabeth does continue to judge him and, more seriously, he accepts those judgements. Furthermore, John judges himself, and both John and Elizabeth pronounce these judgements about John's goodness, not in terms of divine grace or inherent humanness, but in terms of the kinds of superficial, worldly actions (in this case, silence and martyrdom) which have caused Elizabeth to misjudge John in the past. "Yet you've not confessed till now. That speak goodness in you," Elizabeth says to John as he is deciding whether or not to give a false confession; while John imagines that he himself is capable of estimating his place within the kingdom of God: "It is a pretense, Elizabeth," he says of his decision to hang for a crime which he has not committed:

> I cannot mount the gibbet like a saint. It is a fraud. I am not that man. . . . My honesty is broke . . . I am no good man. Nothing's spoiled by giving them this lie that were not rotten long before. . . . Let them that never lied die now to keep their souls. It is a pretense for me, a vanity that will not blind God nor keep my children out of the wind.

Elizabeth immediately confirms John in his belief that he is his own judge: "There be no higher judge under Heaven than Proctor is," she exclaims; and she recurs to her martyristic definition of goodness: "I never knew such goodness in the world."

What is wrong with John's decision to confess, as it is presented in the play, is not only that it is a lie, though this of course is crucial, but more subtly that it is based on a definition of "saint"-hood which is a heretical offence against Proctor's own faith, a definition which depends upon setting oneself up as one's own judge, judging one's works and outer manifestations as evidences of sanctification or damnation. John confesses, not to his true sin, but to a sin he did not commit; not to his God, but to a community of men. In a sense, however, he does commit the sin of demonry when he thus falsely confesses, for he veritably signs a pact with the devil the moment he chooses both to lie and to inaugurate himself as his own judge, his own God as it were. We might even say that he has already begun the process of "devil worship" earlier in the play when he cries out in court that "God is dead", or when he damns the Deputy Governor; and he extends that position later when he damns the village.

But the crisis of faith is further compounded when John refuses to sign the confession and thus assumes a stance of total silence. For Proctor covenants himself with the devil a second time when he refuses to sign, not because he ought to have signed what is a damning and false document, but because his refusal to sign it has more to do with protecting his "good name" than it does with the more noble virtues which the deed pretends to express. It has more to do, in other words, with precisely that same mistaken sense of his own authority and his own ability to project outwardly as a name the inner components of spirit.

The matter of the "good name" is a tricky issue in the play. On the one hand, the "good name" is as important to the playwright as it is to the protagonist. On the other, as again "the playwriting part" of Miller seems eminently aware, attention to one's good name represents an inability to separate inner goodness from outer goodness. In a phrase, the Puritan Proctor has confused "goodness" with a "good name," and this is a confusion, Miller suggests, which we must avoid at all costs. After all, it is also to protect John's good name that Elizabeth perjures herself in court and, in not confessing her real reasons for firing Abigail Williams, effectively ensures John's death ("She only thought to save my name," says John). And we cannot forget Reverend Parris's and Abigail Williams's concern for their good names in act 1. Goodness for John and Elizabeth, and for their community, is identical with one's worldly deeds, with one's good name. "Now I do think I see some shred of goodness in John Proctor," says John of his final refusal to confess to witchcraft to which he has no reason to confess.

He cannot see that his goodness pre-dates this decision, that it was implanted by his God despite his sinfulness.

Proctor's silence, Miller is suggesting, like his desire to confess, does not represent spiritual valour. Indeed, silence itself, rather than representing a virtue, is associated throughout the play with a lack of human feeling and warmth, with a lack of charity, we might say. It is silence, for example, that causes Elizabeth to indict John of continued unfaithfulness in act 2. It is silence which is directly responsible for Abby's not being seen for the whore that she is; silence which finally seals John's doom when Elizabeth refuses to confess the adultery in court; silence which encourages Proctor on his path to martyrdom: "PROCTOR: I cannot mount the gibbet like a saint. . . . [ELIZABETH] *is silent.*" Furthermore, silence is connected, throughout the play, by both John and Danforth, with a stony coldness. "[Y]our justice would freeze beer!" John says to Elizabeth in the scene I have already quoted; "Are you a stone?" Danforth asks her; and John's last rebellious advice to Elizabeth is to "show a stony heart and sink them with it." Giles Corey is pressed to death between stones because of his silence. Coldness and silence, furthermore, are very likely what prompted John's adultery in the first place. "It needs a cold wife to prompt lechery," Elizabeth confesses; "suspicion kissed you when I did. . . . It were a cold house I kept!" And coldness, of course, is also associated with the presence of the devil (see act 3). What Miller seems to be getting at is that silence itself may be a kind of presumption, a kind of pride. It may be a way of asserting one's control over events and their meanings by refusing to respond to the humanness of a human situation (note Elizabeth's silent smiles in act 2 which are associated with her preserving her dignity). Hence, silence is associated with the condition of a stone, because it denies the importance of human communication. Silence, ultimately, divorces the individual from true repentance and true charity, either to other human beings or, more seriously, to their God.

Miller has created a true dilemma for Proctor, a literally damned-if-you-do, damned-if-you-don't situation. Both Proctor's confession and his silence represent a misunderstanding of the terms of divine grace, a mistaken worldly pride, and a commitment to external signs and symbols. Hence, Proctor's fate is sealed, not by his deeds, but by a mind-set which does not allow him to view himself or his actions charitably and thus truly. But this dilemma exists only because the Puritans, Proctor included, had identified saintedness with external goodness, a good name. Goodness, Miller implies, is a purely spiritual, inward state. It is not subject to the laws and dictates of men. In Miller's view, Senator McCarthy and judges Danforth and Hathorne were not the major enemies of American liberty. Moral absolutism, pride, contempt, and a marked tendency to see outward signs as evidence of inner being—these McCarthy-like, Puritan-like qualities—were the opponents of liberty, and they characterized victim as well as victimizer. The reason that McCarthy and the Puritan judges were able to hold court in America was that the Americans judged themselves as their dictators would judge them. The dilemma of John Proctor, then, was the dilemma of America itself. As Miller put it in his introduction to Proctor: "These people had no ritual for the washing away of sins. It is another trait we inherited from them, and it has helped to discipline us as well as to breed hypocrisy among us." John and Elizabeth Proctor, like many other Puritans, perhaps like many other Americans, assumed a priori that they were sinful and thus worthless. Therefore they misread and misjudged their lives' experiences. They judged themselves guilty and were willing to accept the verdict of guilty by others. Most frightening for the nation, this self-destructive attitude of guilt had become institutionalized in the American theocracy, and when it was given power, these qualities which defined the victim became the instruments which supported and strengthened the oppressor. Neither the Proctors nor the Puritan elders, neither the American public nor the McCarthyites, were willing to recognize that only the moral authority of God or of some code larger than man (a secular equivalent of God) was absolute and binding. They had allowed a concept of visible sanctity to outweigh their commitment to inner grace; they had preferred their federal theology to their Calvinist religion. Miller points to this problem very precisely when he has Proctor naïvely demand that he be able to "speak" his "heart." Parris retorts "*in a fury* What, are we Quakers? We are not Quakers here yet, Mr. Proctor. And you may tell that to your followers!" Miller here recalls the antinomian crisis in Puritan New England which, like the witchcraft trials, brought to the surface an inherent tension between the Puritans' strict Calvinist faith and their federal theology; the tension between an invisible covenant between man and God, eternal and unbreakable, and a visible covenant, highly perishable, between God and the people's religious and political institutions. Outward forms, names, and institutions had come to be more cherished than the sanctity of an individual soul, even to the Proctors, who perish as a consequence of what must be viewed not only as apostasy but as human hubris.

How are human beings, in Miller's view, to arrive at moral truth? Tom Driver has argued that:

Miller's strident moralism is a good example of what happens when ideals must be maintained in an atmosphere of humanistic relativism. There being no objective good or evil, and no imperative other than conscience, man himself must be made to bear the full burden of creating his values and living up to them. The immensity of this task is beyond human capacity.

"Strident moralism," however, is just what Miller is attacking in the play; and he does not leave us in an amorphous chaos of "humanistic relativism" with "no imperative other than conscience." For what he discovers in his investigations of history is a moral order larger and more adaptive than any formulation at which a single individual could arrive, an order which is analogous to the Puritan perception of God, and which is defined first and foremost by a recognition of one's own defective moral faculties and therefore of one's utter dependence upon the charity and good will which issue from God (if one is a Puritan) and/or from a similar recognition about themselves on the parts of others (whether one is a Puritan or a twentieth-century American). Morality, Miller suggests, is dependent upon recognizing and accepting our humanness—an acknowledgement which neither Proctor nor Parris nor any of the Puritans is willing to make. After all, the whole hysteria starts because Parris is incapable of dismissing his daughter's and his niece's juvenile midnight escapade for the child's play that it really is. Proctor's crime mirrors the crime of the children; his relentless accusations of himself are a version of Parris's inhuman persecution of the innocents.

According to Miller, our knowledge of morality, our ability to accommodate the imperfect humanness which defines us all, is to a large extent synonymous with our knowledge of history itself. History for Miller is not a judgemental catalogue of instances of human sinfulness. Rather, it is an exploration of the core reasons for human sinfulness—reasons such as guilt, pride, and the desire to render judgement, to see oneself as one of the elect— which allows sympathy for the human dilemma none the less. Miller searches deep into American history, not to discover a convenient analogy to a contemporary problem, but to indicate the importance of registering the relativity and subjectivity of moral justice within the *absolute* moral principles of charity and humility and forgiveness. "It is as impossible," Miller claims:

for most men to conceive of a morality without sin as of an earth without "sky." Since 1692 a great but superficial change has wiped out God's beard and the Devil's horns, but the world is still gripped between two diametrically opposed absolutes. The concept of unity, in which positive and negative are attributes of

the same force, in which good and evil are relative, ever-changing,
and always joined to the same phenomenon—such a concept is
still reserved to the physical sciences and to the few who have
grasped *the history of ideas*. [emphasis added]

History, Miller is claiming, can provide both a sense of moral relativity and
a set of values which enable us to behave morally within that relativity. This
is what "the history of ideas" gives us, historical consciousness and historical knowledge thus becoming necessary prerequisites for moral behaviour.
It is not that Miller does not believe in the devil: "Like Reverend Hale and
the others on this stage, we conceive the Devil as a necessary part of a
respectable cosmology." As he argues in his introduction: "I believe . . .
that, from whatever cause, a dedication to evil, not mistaking it for good,
but knowing it as evil and loving it as evil, is possible in human beings who
appear agreeable and normal. I think now that one of the hidden weaknesses of our whole approach to dramatic psychology is our inability to face
this fact—to conceive, in effect, of Iago." But this is the point exactly: that
for Miller, evil is more primary than the devil who incorporates it. Satan
indeed exists, but as an Iago of the self who is self-created. Thus, Miller puts
the emphasis of his play on the importance of self-awareness, the recognition of evil within oneself, and the acknowledgement that this evil may be
projected onto others through no fault of theirs.

When Proctor instructs Abby to "[w]ipe it out of mind," and when he
falsifies history by claiming that "[w]e never touched," he is already making
himself ready prey to the devil's wiles, because he is denying, on a conscious
level, the original sin and human fallenness—the evil—which are in fact a
part of his nature, and for which, subconsciously, he is already punishing
himself. He is, in other words, being dishonest with himself, and with Abby,
and with Elizabeth as well, as Elizabeth makes clear for us in their long
conversation in act 2. When Proctor thus tries to wipe clean the slate of
history and thereby denies to his own consciousness the necessary lessons of
his own experience, of his own history, he excludes the possibility for integrated consciousness of his goodness as coexistent with his sinfulness, of
his salvation despite his evil.

The situation could not be more dangerous. As a consequence of his
black-and-white morality, Proctor does not see that the Puritans' crimes
against humanity, against himself, constitute versions of his own crimes
against himself. He misunderstands his guilt and therefore misadministers
his punishment. Proctor suffers from a misconceived sense of self in which
he is either wholly saved or wholly damned. Because he fails to read the

historical record, either about himself or about his community, he does not understand that humankind has been defined from the beginning of human history, in the Bible itself, by a curious admixture of good and evil, and that humankind misjudges morality when it ignores the morally vague context of human experience. Since Adam's fall, our relationship with the devil has been much closer than any of us would like to admit, and there are none among us who might not be charged, with a certain degree of truthfulness, with covenanting himself to the devil. This state of affairs is indeed why God has bestowed His grace upon mankind, why He has sacrificed His son.

By writing a historical drama, Miller is asking us to turn to the historical record in order to understand the ambiguous and changing nature of morality. He is evoking our sympathies for characters whose world-view and beliefs are totally different from our own, thus enabling us to do precisely what the Puritans themselves were unable to do—to accept the diversity of opinions, the variety of perceptions, the mixture of bad and good which characterize the human community.

Above all, however, Miller is making a statement about the relationship between objective fact and subjective fiction, or rather, about the existence of subjective fiction within objective fact and vice versa. *The Crucible* not only emphasizes the importance of sympathy in human relationships, but explores why sympathy must be a component of those relationships, not only if we are to see morally, but if we are to see at all. For historical fiction has the unique advantage of insisting upon the realness of the world with which it deals fictively, while simultaneously acknowledging that the world which it is now representing is a consequence as much of the readers' or viewers' subjective perceptions as of any objective fact or reality. In historical drama, the paradoxical relationship between fancy and fact is even more vivid than in written fiction, for the realness of actors enacting a history which has been fictionalized and put on the stage has, from Shakespeare on, inevitably raised its own theoretical arguments about the world and the play. "No one can really know what their lives were like," Miller begins the play. And yet he proceeds to convince us of exactly what their lives were like, as they themselves confronted what was knowable and unknowable, what was fact and fiction, in life itself.

In the case of a historical drama on the Salem witchcraft trials, the historical and literary interest found a coincidence of purpose and meaning that was startling in the extreme. For the issue of the witchcraft trials is precisely the question of the proportion of fiction to fact in our perceptions of the world; and the lesson is what can happen when individuals forget the limits of their own optical and moral senses, and fail to sympathize with fellow citizens suffering from the same impossibility of separating the imaginary from the real. Furthermore, by casting upon his contemporary audience the spectre of Salem, and pretending that Salem is contemporary America, Miller is asking us to recognize the elements of self within our projections of the devil, the subjectivity which ever colours our knowledge of the objective world.

The Crucible, then, by the very procedures which define its dramatic art, enforces upon us a recognition of the difficulty of distinguishing between the subjective and the objective, between the spectre and the witch. Hence, the play invokes our sympathy for the actors of a tragedy who viewed their lives from much the same complicated perspective by which an audience views a play. The play, in other words, imitates the situation of the Puritans, who witnessed their world as the unfolding of a drama in which external events represented internal realities. But whereas the Puritans failed to recognize the fictionality of that dramatic performance in which their lives consisted, Miller's play, as a play, enforces our awareness of the fiction. It insists that life (i.e., history) and literature are both spectres of consciousness, ours or someone else's, projections of the imagination. The Puritans' principal failing, as it emerges in the play, was their inability to accord to each other, even to themselves, the privacy and individuality which are not simply human rights but inherent features of perception itself. By extending our imaginations over centuries of difference, by identifying with the ghosts which are the past and the ghosts in which the past itself believed, we attain to the sympathetic imaginations, the spiritual charity, which the Puritans could not achieve.

Chronology

1915   Born October 17 in New York City, second son of Isadore and Augusta Miller.

1929   Depression causes financial difficulties in father's clothing business. Family moves to Brooklyn.

1934   Enters the University of Michigan, Ann Arbor. Studies journalism.

1936   First play, *Honors at Dawn*, produced. Wins Hopwood Awards in Drama for *No Villain* (1936) and *Honors at Dawn* (1937), and Theatre Guild Bureau of New Plays Award for *They Too Arise*.

1938   Receives Bachelor of Arts from University of Michigan. Begins work with the Federal Theatre Project.

1940   Marries Mary Grace Slattery.

1944   Visits army camps collecting material for screenplay, *The Story of G.I. Joe. Situation Normal* (prose account of this tour) published. *The Man Who Had All the Luck* published and produced in New York; wins Theatre Guild National Prize.

1945   Novel, *Focus*, published.

1947   *All My Sons* produced and published in New York; wins New York Drama Critics' Circle Award.

1949   *Death of a Salesman* published and produced; wins Pulitzer Prize and N.Y. Critics' Circle Award.

1950   Adaptation of Ibsen's *An Enemy of the People* produced.

1953   *The Crucible* produced and published.

1954   Is refused passport by State Department to attend opening of *The Crucible* in Brussels.

1955   *A Memory of Two Mondays* and the one-act version of *A View from the Bridge* produced and published in New York.

1956   Two-act version of *A View from the Bridge* produced in London. Divorces Mary Slattery. Appears before House Un-American Activities Committee. Marries Marilyn Monroe.

1957   Convicted of contempt of Congress for refusing to name suspected communists. *Collected Plays* published.

1958   Conviction reversed by Supreme Court. Elected to the National Arts and Letters Institute.

1960   Filming of *The Misfits*. Separates from Marilyn Monroe.

1961   *The Misfits* released. Divorces Marilyn Monroe. *The Misfits* published as a novel.

1962   Marries Austrian-born photographer Ingeborg Morath. Birth of daughter Rebecca Augusta Miller.

1964   *After the Fall* and *Incident at Vichy* produced by the Lincoln Center Repertory Theatre.

1965   Elected International President of PEN (Poets, Essayists, and Novelists).

1967   *I Don't Need You Any More*, a collection of short stories, published.

1968   *The Price* published and produced in New York. Serves as delegate to Democratic National Convention.

1969   *In Russia* published with Inge Morath.

1970   *Fame* produced in New York.

1972   *The Creation of the World and Other Business* produced in New York. Serves as delegate to the Democratic National Convention.

1974   *Up from Paradise* (musical version of *The Creation of the World*) produced in Ann Arbor, Michigan.

1977   *The Archbishop's Ceiling* produced at the Kennedy Center in Washington, D.C. *In the Country* published with Inge Morath.

1978   Visits China with Inge Morath. *The Theater Essays of Arthur Miller* published.

1980   *The American Clock* produced in New York. *Playing for Time* presented on television.

1982   Two one-acts, *Some Kind of Love Story* and *Elegy for a Lady*, open at the Long Wharf Theater in New Haven.

1983   Directs *Death of a Salesman* in China with Chinese cast.

1984   Revival of *Death of a Salesman* opens on Broadway with Dustin Hoffman as Willy Loman.

1985   Broadcast of 1984 production of *Death of a Salesman* on television.

Contributors

HAROLD BLOOM, Sterling Professor of the Humanities at Yale University, is the author of *The Anxiety of Influence, Poetry and Repression*, and many other volumes of literary criticism. His forthcoming study, *Freud: Transference and Authority*, attempts a full-scale reading of all of Freud's major writings. A MacArthur Prize Fellow, he is general editor of five series of literary criticism published by Chelsea House.

RAYMOND WILLIAMS, Judith F. Wilson Professor of Drama at Cambridge University, is among the most influential British Marxist critics of literature. His books include *Culture and Society, The Long Revolution*, and *The Country and the City*.

TOM F. DRIVER is Professor of Theology and Literature at Union Theological Seminary in New York City. He is the author of *The Sense of History in Greek and Shakespearean Drama*, and *Romantic Quest and Modern Query: A History of the Modern Theater*, and *Jean Genet*.

ESTHER MERLE JACKSON is Professor of Theater and Drama at the University of Wisconsin, Madison. She is the author of *The Broken World of Tennessee Williams* and of studies of Maxwell Anderson and Imamu Amiri Baraka (LeRoi Jones).

CLINTON W. TROWBRIDGE is Professor of English at Dowling College in Oakdale, New York. He has published articles on Salinger, Bellow, and Flannery O'Connor.

ORM ÖVERLAND is Professor of American Literature at the University at Bergen, Norway. He is the editor of the journal *American Studies in Scandinavia* and the author of *The Making of an American Classic: James Fenimore Cooper's "The Prairie,"* and *America Perceived: A View from Abroad in the Twentieth Century*.

DENNIS WELLAND is Professor of American Literature at the University of Manchester. He founded and for ten years edited the *Journal of American Studies*, and edited and contributed to *The USA: A Companion to American Studies*. He is the author of *Mark Twain and England* and *Wilfred Owen: A Critical Study*.

LEONARD MOSS is Professor of Comparative Literature at the State University of New York, Genesee. He has written on Aeschylus, Seneca, Milton, and Kafka.

NEIL CARSON is Associate Professor of English at the University of Guelph in Canada.

C. W. E. BIGSBY is Senior Lecturer in American Literature at the University of East Anglia. He is the author of *Confrontation and Commitment* and *Dada and Surrealism,* and has edited these collections of essays: *Edward Albee, The Black American Writer,* and *Superculture: The Influence of American Popular Culture on Europe.*

E. MILLER BUDICK is Senior Lecturer in American Studies and English Literature at The Hebrew University of Jerusalem. He has written on Edgar Allen Poe, Emily Dickinson, Nathaniel Hawthorne, and William Cullen Bryant.

Bibliography

Aarnes, William. "Tragic Form and the Possibility of Meaning in *Death of a Salesman.*" *Furman Study* (1984): 57–80.

Bates, Barclay W. "The Lost Past in *Death of a Salesman.*" *Modern Drama* 11 (1968): 164–72.

Bentley, Eric. "Back to Broadway." *Theatre Arts* 33 (1949): 10–19.

———. "On the Waterfront." *What Is Theatre?* New York: Beacon, 1956.

Bermel, Albert. "Right, Wrong and Mr. Miller." *New York Times*, 14 April 1968.

Bettina, Sister M. "Willy Loman's Brother Ben: Tragic Insight in *Death of a Salesman.*" *Modern Drama* 4 (1962): 409–12.

Bigsby, C. W. E. "Arthur Miller." In *Confrontation and Commitment: A Study of Contemporary American Drama.* Columbia: University of Missouri Press, 1967.

Blumberg, Paul. "Sociology and Social Literature: Work Alienation in the Plays of Arthur Miller." *American Quarterly* 21 (1969): 291–310.

Bonnet, Jean M. "Society vs. the Individual in Arthur Miller's *The Crucible.*" *English Studies* 63 (1982): 32–36.

Boruch, Marianne. "Miller and Things." *Literary Review* 24 (1981): 548–61.

Brashear, William R. "The Empty Bench: Morality, Tragedy, and Arthur Miller." *Michigan Quarterly Review* 5 (1966): 270–78.

Brater, Enoch. "Ethics and Ethnicity in the Plays of Arthur Miller." In *From Hester St. to Hollywood: the Jewish-American Stage and Screen,* edited by Sarah Blacker Cohen. Bloomington: Indiana University Press, 1983.

Bronson, David. "*An Enemy of the People*: A Key to Arthur Miller's Art and Ethics." *Comparative Drama* 2 (1968): 229–47.

Broussard, Louis. *American Drama: Contemporary Allegory from Eugene O'Neill to Tennessee Williams.* Norman: University of Oklahoma Press, 1962.

Brucker, Richard T. "Willy Loman and *The Soul of a New Machine*: Technology and the Common Man." *Jewish American Studies* 17(3) (1983): 325–36.

Brustein, Robert. "Arthur Miller's Mea Culpa." *The New Republic*, 8 February 1964: 26–30.

Calarco, N. Joseph. "Production as Criticism: Miller's *The Crucible.*" *Educational Theatre Journal* 29 (1977): 354–61.

Centola, Steven R. "Confrontation with the Other: Alienation in the Works of Arthur Miller and Jean-Paul Sartre." *Journal of Evolutionary Psychology* 1, 2 (1984): 1–11.

————. "Unblessed Rage for Order: Arthur Miller's *After the Fall.*" *Arizona Quarterly* 39 (1983): 62–70.

Cohn, Ruby. "The Articulate Victims of Arthur Miller." *Dialogue in American Drama,* 68–96. Bloomington: Indiana University Press, 1971.

Collins, Anthony R. "Arthur Miller and the Judgement of God." *South Central Bulletin* 42 (1982): 120–24.

Corrigan, Robert W., ed. *Arthur Miller: A Collection of Critical Essays.* Englewood Cliffs, N.J.: Prentice-Hall, 1969.

Dworkin, Martin. "Miller and Ibsen." *Humanist* 11 (1951): 110–15.

Ferres, John H., ed. *Twentieth Century Interpretations of* The Crucible. Englewood Cliffs, N.J.: Prentice-Hall, 1972.

Flaxman, Seymour L. "The Debt of Williams and Miller to Ibsen and Strindberg." *Comparative Literature Studies,* Special Advance Issue (1963).

Foulkes, A.P. *Literature and Propaganda.* London: Methuen, 1983.

Freedman, Morris. "Bertolt Brecht and American Social Drama." *The Moral Impulse: Modern Drama from Ibsen to the Present,* 99–114. Carbondale: Southern Illinois University Press, 1967.

Ganz, Arthur. "The Silence of Arthur Miller." *Drama Survey* 3 (1963): 224–37.

Gassner, John. *Form and Idea in Modern Theatre.* New York: Dryden, 1956.

Gollub, Christian-Albrecht. "Interview with Arthur Miller." *Michigan Quarterly Review* 16 (1977): 121–41.

Hayman, Ronald. *Arthur Miller.* London: Heinemann, 1970.

————. "Arthur Miller: Between Sartre and Society." *Encounter* 37 (1971): 73–79.

Hays, Peter L. "Arthur Miller and Tennessee Williams." *Essays in Literature* 4 (1977): 239–49.

Heilman, Robert Bechtold. "Arthur Miller." *The Iceman, the Arsonist, and the Troubled Agent: Tragedy and Melodrama on the Modern Stage,* 142–64. Seattle: University of Washington Press, 1973.

Hurd, Gyles R. "Angels and Anxieties in Miller's *A View from the Bridge.*" *Notes on Contemporary Literature* 13, no. 9 (1983): 4–6.

Hurrell, John D., ed. *Two Modern American Tragedies: Reviews and Criticism of* Death of a Salesman *and* A Streetcar Named Desire. New York: Scribners, 1961.

Hynes, Joseph A. "Arthur Miller and the Impasse of Naturalism." *South Atlantic Quarterly* 62 (1963): 327–34.

Inserillo, Charles R. "Wish and Desire: Two Poles of the Imagination in the Drama of Arthur Miller and T. S. Eliot." *Xavier University Studies* 1 (1962): 247–58.

Jacobson, Irving. "Christ, Pygmalion, and Hitler in *After the Fall.*" *Essays in Literature* 2 (1974): 12–27.

Koon, Helen W., ed. Death of a Salesman: *A Collection of Critical Essays.* Englewood Cliffs, N.J.: Prentice-Hall, 1983.

Koppenhaver, Allen J. "*The Fall* and After: Albert Camus and Arthur Miller." *Modern Drama* 9 (1966): 206–9.

Lowenthal, Lawrence D. "Arthur Miller's *Incident at Vichy:* A Sartrean Interpretation." *Modern Drama* 18 (1975): 29–41.

Martin, Robert A. "Arthur Miller's *The Crucible*: Background and Sources." *Modern Drama* 20 (1977): 279–92.

————, ed. *Arthur Miller: New Perspectives.* Englewood Cliffs, N.J.: Prentice-Hall, 1982.

McGill, William. "The Crucible of History: Arthur Miller's John Proctor." *New England Quarterly* 54, no. 2 (1981): 258–64.

McMahon, Helen. "Arthur Miller's Common Man: The Problem of the Realistic and the Mythic." *Drama and Theatre* 10 (1972): 128–33.

Meserve, Walter J., ed. *The Merrill Studies in* "Death of a Salesman." Columbus, Ohio: Merrill, 1972.

Mesher, David R. "Arthur Miller's *Focus*: The First American Novel of the Holocaust?" *Judaism* 29, no. 4 (1980): 469–78.

Miles, O. Thomas. "Three Authors in Search of a Character." *Personalist* 46 (1965): 65–72.

Miller, Jeanne-Marie A. "Odets, Miller, and Communism." *College Language Association Journal* 19 (1976): 484–93.

Nelson, Benjamin. *Arthur Miller.* London: Owen, 1970.

Noevels, Diane Long. "*Death of a Salesman* as Psychomachics." *Journal of American Culture* 1 (1978): 632–37.

O'Neal, Michael J. "History, Myths, and Name Magic in Arthur Miller's *The Crucible*." *Clio* 12, no. 2 (1983): 111–22.

Partridge, C. J. "*The Crucible.*" Oxford: Basil Blackwell, 1971.

Popkin, Henry. "Arthur Miller: The Strange Encounter." *Sewanee Review* 68 (1960): 34–60.

————. "Arthur Miller Out West." *Commentary* 31 (1961): 433–36.

Press, David. "Arthur Miller's *The Misfits*: The Western Gunned Down." *Studies in the Humanities* 8, no. 1: 41–44.

Prudhoe, John. "Arthur Miller and the Tradition of Tragedy." *English Studies* 43 (1962): 430–39.

Shaw, Patrick. "The Ironic Characterization of Bernard in *Death of a Salesman*." *Notes on Contemporary Literature* 11, no. 3 (1981): 12.

Rajuhishnan, V. "After Commitment: An Interview with Arthur Miller." *Theatre Journal* 32: 196–204.

Tynan, Kenneth. *Curtains.* New York: Atheneum, 1961.

Vogel, Dan. "Willy Tyrannos." *The Three Masks of American Tragedy,* 91–102. Baton Rouge: Louisiana State University Press, 1974.

Wattenberg, Richard. "Staging William James's 'World of Pure Experience': Arthur Miller's 'Death of a Salesman.' " *Theatre Annual* 38 (1983): 49–64.

Weales, Gerald., ed. *Arthur Miller: Death of a Salesman.* New York: Viking, 1967.ern Drama 20 (1977): 279–92.

Acknowledgments

"Arthur Miller: An Overview" (originally entitled "Arthur Miller") by Raymond Williams from *Drama: From Ibsen to Brecht* by Raymond Williams, © 1952 by Raymond Williams. Reprinted by permission of the author, Chatto & Windus Ltd. and Oxford University Press.

"Strength and Weakness in Arthur Miller" by Tom Driver from *The Tulane Drama Review* 4, no. 4 (May 1960), © 1960 by the *Tulane Drama Review*. Reprinted by permission.

"*Death of a Salesman:* Tragic Myth in the Modern Theatre" by Esther Merle Jackson from *College Language Association Journal* 7, no. 1 (September 1963), © 1963 by the College Language Association. Reprinted by permission.

"Arthur Miller: Between Pathos and Tragedy" by Clinton W. Trowbridge from *Modern Drama* 10, no. 3 (December 1967), © 1967 by University of Toronto, Graduate Centre for the Study of Drama. Reprinted by permission of *Modern Drama*.

"The Action and Its Significance: Arthur Miller's Struggle with Dramatic Form" by Orm Överland from *Modern Drama* 18, no. 1 (March 1975), © 1975 by University of Toronto, Graduate Centre for the Study of Drama. Reprinted by permission of *Modern Drama*.

"The Drama of Forgiveness" (originally entitled "*After the Fall*") by Dennis Welland from *Arthur Miller: A Study of His Plays* by Dennis Miller, © 1979 by Dennis Welland. Reprinted by permission of Methuen & Co. Ltd., London.

"The Perspective of a Playwright" by Leonard Moss from *Arthur Miller* by Leonard Moss, © 1980 by Twayne Publishers, a division of G. K. Hall & Co. Reprinted by permission.

"*A View from the Bridge* and the Expansion of Vision" (originally entitled "*A View from the Bridge*") by Neil Carson from *Arthur Miller* by Neil Carson, © 1982 by Neil Carson. Reprinted by permission of the author and Grove Press, Inc.

"Drama from a Living Center" (originally entitled "Arthur Miller") by C. W. E. Bigsby from *A Critical Introduction to Twentieth-Century American Drama 2: Tennessee Williams, Arthur Miller, Edward Albee* by C. W. E. Bigsby, © 1984

155

by C. W. E. Bigsby. Reprinted by permission of the author and Cambridge University Press.

"History and Other Spectres in *The Crucible*" (originally entitled "History and Other Spectres in Arthur Miller's *The Crucible*") by E. Miller Budick from *Modern Drama* 28, no. 4 (December 1985), © 1985 by the University of Toronto, Graduate Centre for the Study of Drama. Reprinted by permission of *Modern Drama*.

Index